# Level 1 • Part 2
# Integrated Chinese
# 中文听说读写

## WORKBOOK Simplified Characters

**Third Edition**

**THIRD EDITION BY**

Yuehua Liu and Tao-chung Yao
Nyan-Ping Bi, Yaohua Shi, Liangyan Ge, Yea-fen Chen

**ORIGINAL EDITION BY**

Tao-chung Yao and Yuehua Liu
Yea-fen Chen, Liangyan Ge, Nyan-Ping Bi,
Xiaojun Wang, Yaohua Shi

 CHENG & TSUI COMPANY
Boston

16 15 14 13 12 11 10      2 3 4 5 6 7 8 9 10

Published by
Cheng & Tsui Company, Inc.
25 West Street
Boston, MA 02111-1213 USA
Fax (617) 426-3669
www.cheng-tsui.com
"Bringing Asia to the World"™


ISBN 978-0-88727-674-3

Cover Design: studioradia.com

Cover Photographs: Man with map © Getty Images; Shanghai skyline © David Pedre/iStockphoto; Building with masks © Wu Jie; Night market © Andrew Buko. Used by permission.

Interior Design: Wanda España, Wee Design

Illustrations: 洋洋兔动漫


The *Integrated Chinese* series includes books, workbooks, character workbooks, audio products, multimedia products, teacher's resources, and more. Visit www.cheng-tsui.com for more information on the other components of *Integrated Chinese*.


Printed in Canada.

# Contents

# Preface to the Third Edition

This new Workbook accompanies the third edition of *Integrated Chinese* (*IC*). In response to teachers' feedback and requests, the new *Integrated Chinese Level 1* includes 20 lessons (10 in Part 1 and 10 in Part 2), instead of 23 lessons as in the earlier editions. The format of the third edition Workbook remains largely unchanged. For maximum flexibility in pacing, each lesson is divided into two parts corresponding to the two sections of the lesson in the textbook. The exercises cover the language form and the four language skills of listening, speaking, reading, and writing.

We have also made several improvements and added new features in the new edition of the Workbook.

## Three Modes of Communication Clearly Labeled

We would like to point out that our exercises cover the three modes of communication as explained in "Standards for Foreign Language Learning in the 21st Century": interpretive, interpersonal and presentational. We have labeled the exercises as interpretive, interpersonal or presentational wherever applicable.

## More Authentic Materials Incorporated

To build a bridge between the pedagogical materials used in the classroom and the materials that the student will face in the target language environment, we have included authentic materials in the exercises for all lessons.

## New Illustrations Added

To make the exercises more interesting and appealing, we have added many illustrations to the exercises. These visual images increase the variety of exercise types, and also stimulate the student to answer questions directly in Chinese without going through the translation process.

# Contextualized Grammar Exercises and Task-Oriented Assignments Provided

The ultimate goal of learning any language is to be able to communicate in that language. With that goal in mind, we pay equal attention to language form and language function, and have created task-based exercises to train the student to handle real life situations using the language accurately and appropriately. We have rewritten many items, especially in the translation section, to provide linguistic context and to reflect the language used in real life.

# Learner-Centered Tasks Included

We believe that the exercises in the Workbook should not only integrate the materials of the Textbook, but also relate to the student's life. We include exercises that simulate daily life with topics and themes that are relevant and personal to the student. We hope these exercises will actively engage students in the subject matter, and keep them interested in the language learning process. Since the world is constantly changing, we also have tried to add exercises that will train the student to meet the needs of today's world, such as writing e-mail messages in Chinese.

# New Rejoinders Added

To help the student develop interpersonal skills, we have added a couple of rejoinders to each lesson. A rejoinder is used to see if the student can answer a question or respond to a remark logically and meaningfully.

# New Exercises for Storytelling Added

To train students to describe what they see and use their language skills to construct narratives, we have added one storytelling exercise to each lesson. This exercise will let the student develop skills for organizing ideas and presenting them in a coherent manner. It also provides practice in using transitional elements and cohesive devices to make the story progress smoothly and logically. This exercise is suitable for either speaking or writing. The teacher can ask the student to submit the story as a written exercise and/or ask the student to make an oral presentation in class.

# New Review Exercises Supplied

Every five lessons, a cumulative review unit is available to those students who wish to do a periodic progress check. The review units do not introduce any new learning materials, and can be included in or excluded from any curriculum planning, according to individual needs. These units are flexible, short, and useful as a review tool.

We would like to take this opportunity to thank all those who have given us feedback in the past, and extend our sincere gratitude to Professor Zheng-sheng Zhang of San Diego State University for his invaluable editorial comments and to Ms. Laurel Damashek at Cheng & Tsui for her support throughout the production process. We welcome your comments and feedback; please send any observations or suggestions to **editor@cheng-tsui.com.**

# Preface to the Second Edition

In designing the Level One workbook exercises for *Integrated Chinese*, we strove to give equal emphasis to the students' listening, speaking, reading and writing skills. There are different difficulty levels in order to provide variety and flexibility to suit different curriculum needs. Teachers should assign the exercises at their discretion; they should not feel pressured into using all of them and should feel free to use them out of sequence, if appropriate. Moreover, teachers can complement this workbook with their own exercises.

The exercises in each lesson are divided into two parts. The exercises in Part One are for the first dialogue and those in Part Two are for the second dialogue. This way, the two dialogues in each lesson can be taught separately. The teacher can use the first two or three days to teach the first dialogue and ask the students to do all the exercises in Part One, then go on to teach the second dialogue. The teacher can also give two separate vocabulary tests for the two dialogues so as to reduce the pressure of memorizing too many new words at the same time.

## Listening Comprehension

All too often listening comprehension is sacrificed in a formal classroom setting because of time constraints. Students tend to focus their time and energy on the mastery of a few grammar points. This workbook tries to remedy this imbalance by including a substantial number of listening comprehension exercises. There are two categories of listening exercises; both can be done on the students' own time or in the classroom. In either case, it is important to have the instructor review the students' answers for accuracy.

The first category of listening exercises, which is at the beginning of this section, is based on the text of each lesson. For the exercises to be meaningful, students should *first* study the vocabulary list, and *then* listen to the recordings *before* attempting to read the texts. The questions are provided to help students' aural understanding of the texts and to test their reading comprehension.

The second category of listening exercises consists of an audio CD recording of two or more mini-dialogues or narratives. These exercises are designed to give students extra practice on the vocabulary and grammar points introduced in the lesson. Some of the exercises, especially ones that ask students to choose among several possible answers, are significantly more difficult than others. These exercises should be assigned towards the end of the lesson, when the students have become familiar with the content of the lesson.

## Speaking Exercises

Here, too, there are two types of exercises. They are designed for different levels of proficiency within each lesson and should be assigned at the appropriate time.

To help students apply their newly-acquired vocabulary and grammatical understanding to meaningful communication, we first ask them questions related to the dialogues and narratives, and then ask them questions related to their own lives. These questions require a one- or two-sentence answer. By stringing together short questions and answers, students can construct their own mini-dialogues, practice in pairs or take turns asking or answering questions.

Once they have gained some confidence, students can progress to the more difficult questions, where they are invited to express opinions on a number of topics. Typically, these questions are abstract, so they gradually teach

## II. Speaking Exercises

**A.** Answer the questions in Chinese based on the Textbook Dialogue. (INTERPRETIVE/PRESENTATIONAL)

1. How was today's weather in comparison with yesterday's?
2. What was Gao Wenzhong's plan for tomorrow?
3. Where did Gao Xiaoyin read the weather forecast?
4. Why did Gao Xiaoyin tell Gao Wenzhong to change his plan?

**B.** Ask your partner what he/she usually does when the weather is not good. (INTERPERSONAL)

**C.** Check this weekend's weather forecast. Find out if the weather will be nice or not and describe what you plan to do according to the predicted weather conditions. (INTERPRETIVE/PRESENTATIONAL)

## III. Reading Comprehension (INTERPRETIVE)

### A. Building Words

If you combine the *huá* in *huá bīng* with the *shuǐ* in *hē shuǐ*, you have *huá shuǐ*, as seen in #1 below. Can you guess what the word *huá shuǐ* means? Complete this section by providing the characters, the *pinyin*, and the English equivalent of each new word formed this way. You may consult a dictionary if necessary.

|  | new word | *pinyin* | English |
|---|---|---|---|
| 1. "滑冰" 的 "滑" + "喝水" 的 "水" → 滑+水 → | _____ | _____ | _____ |
| 2. "滑冰" 的 "滑" + "下雪" 的 "雪" → 滑+雪 → | _____ | _____ | _____ |
| 3. "学校" 的 "校" + "公园" 的 "园" → 校+园 → | _____ | _____ | _____ |

**4.** "暖和"的"暖"+"天气"的"气"

→   暖+气   →   _____   _____   _____

**5.** "飞机"的"飞"+"看碟"的"碟"

→   飞+碟   →   _____   _____   _____

**B.** Read the following passage and answer the questions.

星期五下午王朋约了李友星期天一起去公园滑冰。可是电视上的天气预报说，星期天的天气不好，会下雪。王朋就给李友打电话，告诉她星期天不去公园了。星期天上午王朋请李友来他的宿舍看碟，可是星期天的天气很好，不但没下雪，而且很暖和。王朋说："以后电视上说会下雪，我们就可以去公园玩儿。电视上说天气很好，我们就只能在家看碟了。"

Questions: (True/False)

(   ) **1.** The story took place in the summer.
(   ) **2.** They had to change their plan for Sunday because of the weather forecast.
(   ) **3.** Wang Peng got the weather forecast from the internet.
(   ) **4.** The forecast predicted that it would snow.
(   ) **5.** Wang Peng was glad that he and Li You were not out on Sunday.
(   ) **6.** According to Wang Peng, the weather forecast is not reliable.

**C.** Read the following passage and answer the questions.

现在已经是一月了，可是不但不下雪，而且很暖和。大家都很高兴，可是小美不太高兴。她问李友："一月的天气怎么跟十月一样啊？什么时候才会冷啊？"李友不懂小美为什么希望天气冷，就去问白英爱，才知道小美上个星期买了一件漂亮的新大衣。

Questions (Multiple Choice)

( )  **1.** The season described in the story is _____.

    **a.** spring
    **b.** summer
    **c.** autumn
    **d.** winter

( )  **2.** Which of the following best describes the current weather conditions?

    **a.** seasonably cold
    **b.** unseasonably warm
    **c.** seasonably rainy
    **d.** unseasonably snowy

( )  **3.** To Li You, Xiaomei's comments on the weather were _____.

    **a.** interesting
    **b.** annoying
    **c.** expected
    **d.** perplexing

( )  **4.** Which of the statements is most likely to be true?

    **a.** Xiaomei knows both Li You and Bai Ying'ai.
    **b.** Xiaomei knows Li You but not Bai Ying'ai.
    **c.** Xiaomei knows neither Li You nor Bai Ying'ai.
    **d.** Xiaomei knows Bai Ying'ai but not Li You.

( )  **5.** According to Bai Ying'ai, Xiaomei is quite eager to _____.

    **a.** experience cold weather
    **b.** experience typical October-like weather
    **c.** wear her new overcoat
    **d.** return her new overcoat

**D.** Answer the following questions based on the authentic material provided.

| 城市 | 天气 | 气温(℃) | 城市 | 天气 | 气温(℃) |
|---|---|---|---|---|---|
| 华盛顿 | | 34~24 | 新德里 | | 35~27 |
| 纽约 | | 32~23 | 德黑兰 | | 39~25 |
| 芝加哥 | | 26~18 | 莫斯科 | | 26~15 |
| 洛杉矶 | | 24~17 | 圣彼得堡 | | 26~15 |
| 旧金山 | | 20~12 | 伊斯坦布尔 | | 30~21 |
| 温哥华 | | 22~11 | 雅典 | | 34~25 |
| 蒙特利尔 | | 26~16 | 维也纳 | | 27~15 |
| 多伦多 | | 28~20 | 日内瓦 | | 28~12 |
| 阿卡波克 | | 24~11 | 法兰克福 | | 25~14 |
| 巴西利亚 | | 25~13 | 柏林 | | 21~11 |
| 里约热内卢 | | 26~17 | 汉堡 | | 20~13 |
| 布宜诺斯艾利斯 | | 12~9 | 巴黎 | | 25~15 |
| 圣地亚哥 | | 11~6 | 里昂 | | 30~18 |
| 东京 | | 31~24 | 曼彻斯特 | | 18~10 |
| 曼谷 | | 33~25 | 伦敦 | | 21~14 |
| 新加坡 | | 29~25 | 斯德哥尔摩 | | 19~12 |
| 吉隆坡 | | 30~23 | 马德里 | | 37~17 |
| 马尼拉 | | 32~25 | 巴塞罗那 | | 29~22 |
| 惠灵顿 | | 13~9 | 米兰 | | 29~18 |
| 悉尼 | | 16~8 | 华沙 | | 23~12 |
| 卡拉奇 | | 33~28 | 开普敦 | | 16~6 |

纽约这一天的天气冷还是暖和？

_____

你还认识哪些城市？

_____

# IV. Writing Exercises

**A.** This is how a retailer touts his merchandise:

我们的东西不但好，而且便宜。

Other selling points:

多、新、好看、好用、男人喜欢，女人喜欢，大人喜欢，小孩喜欢

1._____

2._____

3._____

However, his customers think otherwise:

他们的东西不但不好，而且不便宜。

1._____

2._____

3._____

**B.** Little Wang has become environmentally conscious, and is trying to save energy in any way he can.

EXAMPLE: ✓ ✗

→ 小王以前上网聊天儿，现在不上网聊天儿了。

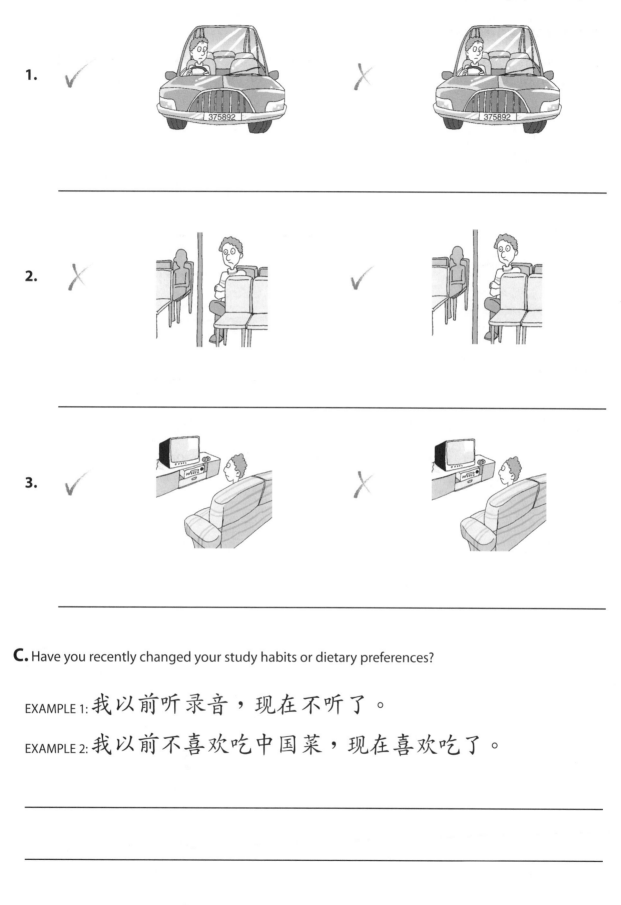

**C.** Have you recently changed your study habits or dietary preferences?

EXAMPLE 1: 我以前听录音，现在不听了。

EXAMPLE 2: 我以前不喜欢吃中国菜，现在喜欢吃了。

_____

_____

_____

## D. Weather Forecast

Here's a weather forecast for New York and Beijing tomorrow. Interpret the forecast to write whether it will snow in each place, and if it will be colder or warmer than the place where you are.

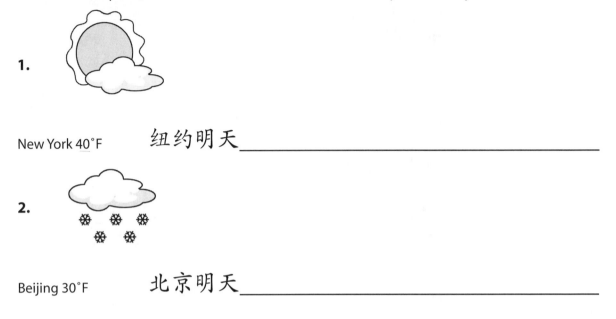

**1.**

New York 40°F        纽约明天_____

**2.**

Beijing 30°F        北京明天_____

**E.** Translate the following into Chinese. (PRESENTATIONAL)

**1.** The weather forecast on the internet just said that it will not only be very cold tomorrow but it will also snow.

_____

_____

**2.** My older sister likes to shop. She bought a white shirt two weeks ago. Last week she bought a pair of blue pants. She liked them very much, so yesterday she bought another pair. She said she would like a pair of black shoes. This afternoon she'll go out shopping again. She really has a lot of money.

_____

_____

_____

_____

_____

**F.** Compare two of your favorite or least favorite celebrities in the same field or profession. Based on your previous knowledge and information you can find online, describe who's younger, taller, richer, who's more beautiful/handsome, and who is better at singing, dancing, playing sports, etc. (PRESENTATIONAL)

## 气象小贴士

今日降旗时刻：19:45

天气：阴有雷阵雨,偏南风2、3级,27至26℃

明日升旗时刻:4:54

天气:多云,偏北风1、2级,22至23℃

### 上下班气象

今天下班：阴有雷阵雨,偏南风2、3级,28至26℃

明天上班:多云,偏北风1、2级,23至25℃

### 穿衣指数

白天适宜穿薄短袖类服装。

### 洗车指数

未来两天有雷阵雨,不适宜洗车。

In addition to a weather forecast, what other advice does this newspaper clipping give?

## PART TWO | Dialogue II: The Weather Here Is Awful

## I. Listening Comprehension

### A. Textbook Dialogue (True/False) (INTERPRETIVE)

( ) **1.** Gao Wenzhong and Bai Ying'ai are talking on the phone.

( ) **2.** Bai Ying'ai is surfing the internet for weather information.

( ) **3.** Gao Wenzhong is moving to California for its good weather.

( ) **4.** Bai Ying'ai is interviewing for a job in New York because she does not like California.

( ) **5.** Bai Ying'ai will cut her trip short because she can't stand the local weather anymore.

### B. Workbook Dialogue (Multiple Choice) (INTERPRETIVE)

( ) **1.** It's been raining since at least yesterday.

( ) **2.** The woman likes rainy weather.

( ) **3.** The woman is from another city.

( ) **4.** The man doesn't care whether the woman stays or not.

( ) **5.** The woman probably would consider watching a different DVD with the man.

### C. Listening Rejoinder (INTERPERSONAL)

In this section, you will hear two speakers talking. After hearing the first speaker, select the best from the four possible responses given by the second speaker.

_____

## II. Speaking Exercises

**A.** Answer the questions in Chinese based on the Textbook Dialogue. (INTERPRETIVE/ PRESENTATIONAL)

1. How did Gao Wenzhong and Bai Ying'ai communicate with each other?

2. Why didn't Bai Ying'ai go out?

3. What kept Bai Ying'ai from going home?

4. Does Bai Ying'ai think that the weather in California is nice? Does she want to go there? Why or why not?

**B.** Ask your partner what his/her favorite city is and to describe what the weather is like there (in each season). (INTERPERSONAL)

# III. Reading Comprehension (INTERPRETIVE)

## A. Building Words

If you combine the *yǔ* in *xià yǔ* with the *yī* in *yīfu*, you have *yǔyī*, as seen in #1 below. Can you guess what the word *yǔyī* means? Complete this section by providing the characters, the *pinyin* and the English equivalent of each new word formed this way. You may consult a dictionary if necessary.

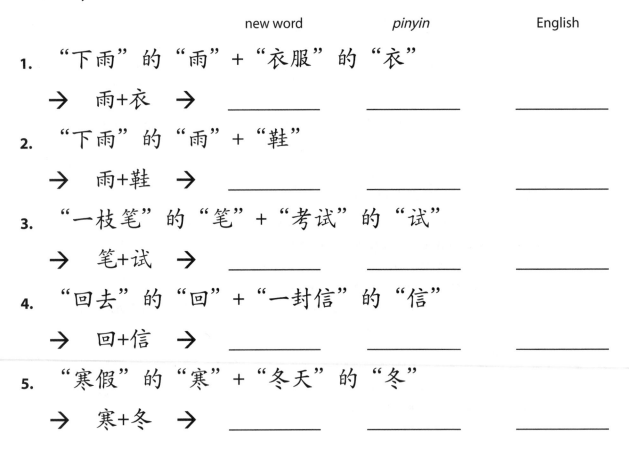

|  | new word | *pinyin* | English |
|---|---|---|---|
| 1. "下雨"的"雨"+"衣服"的"衣" | | | |
| → 雨+衣 → _____ | _____ | _____ | |
| 2. "下雨"的"雨"+"鞋" | | | |
| → 雨+鞋 → _____ | _____ | _____ | |
| 3. "一枝笔"的"笔"+"考试"的"试" | | | |
| → 笔+试 → _____ | _____ | _____ | |
| 4. "回去"的"回"+"一封信"的"信" | | | |
| → 回+信 → _____ | _____ | _____ | |
| 5. "寒假"的"寒"+"冬天"的"冬" | | | |
| → 寒+冬 → _____ | _____ | _____ | |

**B.** Read the passage and answer the questions (True/False).

黄先生以前在加州工作。加州冬天不冷，夏天不热，春天和秋天更舒服。黄先生现在在纽约工作。他说纽约夏天很热，春天秋天也不太舒服，冬天天气更糟糕，不但很冷，而且常常下雪。他约夏小姐这个周末去加州玩儿，夏小姐说加州天气好是好，可是没意思。

( ) **1.** Mr. Huang used to work in California.

( ) **2.** The four seasons were equally comfortable in New York.

( ) **3.** In New York, winter is the worst season.

( ) **4.** Mr. Huang would like to spend a weekend in California.

( ) **5.** Ms. Xia declined Mr. Huang's invitation because she liked the weather in her own city better.

**C.** Read the passage and answer the questions (True/False).

　　谢小姐是北京人，在加州工作。她的爸爸妈妈都在北京，谢小姐常常去看他们。可是她不喜欢夏天回去，因为北京的夏天很热。谢小姐想请她爸爸妈妈夏天到加州来，可是她的爸爸妈妈说，加州好是好，可是那儿的朋友比北京少得多。所以他们觉得北京虽然天气不好，可是比加州更有意思。

( ) 1. 谢小姐的爸爸妈妈常常去加州。

( ) 2. 谢小姐常常在六月或者七月回北京。

( ) 3. 谢小姐的爸爸妈妈在北京有很多朋友。

( ) 4. 谢小姐觉得加州夏天的天气比北京好。

( ) 5. 谢小姐的爸爸妈妈很喜欢北京。

**D.** Read the following dialogue and answer the questions.

（老王和老李打电话聊天。）

老王：老李，我最近工作不忙，想去北京玩儿。

老李：现在是冬天，这儿天气非常冷。

老王：春天呢？

老李：北京春天的天气有的时候也很糟糕！

老王：夏天呢？

老李：夏天比春天更糟糕，不但很热而且常常下雨。

老王：啊，冬天不好，春天不好，夏天也不好，你不希望
我去北京，对吗？

老李：不、不，你是我最好的朋友。我希望你秋天来，因
为北京秋天最舒服。

老王：那好，我秋天去。

Questions: (True/False)

( ) **1.** The telephone conversation took place in the summer.

( ) **2.** Lao Li lives in Beijing.

( ) **3.** According to Lao Li, the best season in Beijing is autumn.

( ) **4.** It is not very cold in winter in Beijing.

( ) **5.** Lao Li doesn't want Lao Wang to come to Beijing.

**E.** This sign indicates that this is a place for _____.

**F.** Answer the following questions based on the visual given.

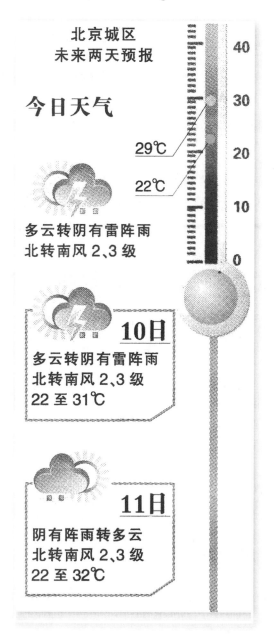

1. 这是哪一个城市的天气预报？ _____

2. 哪一天最热？ _____

3. 这几天会不会下雨？ _____

# IV. Writing Exercises

## A. Building Characters

Form a character by fitting the given components together as indicated. Then provide a word or phrase in which that character appears.

EXAMPLE: a 日 on the left with a 月 on the right: It is the character <u>明</u> as in <u>明天</u>.

1. a 力 on the left with a 口 on the right: It is the character _____ as in _____.

2. a three-dot water radical on the left with the 先 in 先生: It is the character _____

   as in _____.

3. a 女 on the left with a 口 on the right: It is the character _____ as in _____.

4. a 今 on the top with a 心 at the bottom: It is the character _____ as

   in _____.

5. a three-dot water radical on the left with the 票 in 机票 on the right: It is the

   character _____ as in _____.

## B. Shoe shopping

Person A really likes this pair of shoes. She loves the color, the style, the fit, and the comfort, and would like to purchase them. But her mother, Person B, is only concerned about the price. What would you say to A in a diplomatic but honest way if you were B?

EXAMPLE: **A:** 这双鞋的颜色真漂亮。

**B:** 颜色<u>漂亮是漂亮</u>，<u>可是太贵了</u>。

1. **A:** 这双鞋的样子真好看。

   **B:** 样子_____，_____。

2. **A:** 这双鞋的大小真合适。

   **B:** 大小_____，_____。

3.  **A:** 这双鞋真舒服。

    **B:** _____ , _____ 。

**C.** Little Zhang is a true fan of *Harry Potter*. He read it again and again during the winter break. Here's part of the reading log he kept.

| December 26 | December 27 | December 28 | December 29 | December 30 |
|---|---|---|---|---|
| *Harry Potter* | *Harry Potter* | *Harry Potter* | *Harry Potter* | *Harry Potter* |
| ✓ | ✓ | ✗ | ✓ | ✓ |

小张十二月二十六日看了 *Harry Potter* ，十二月二十七日又看

了 *Harry Potter* 。

十二月二十八日 _____

十二月二十九日 _____

十二月三十日 _____

How about you? Are you a fan of *Harry Potter* or any other books, or are you enthusiastic about a particular movie, TV show, sports team, or musician? Write a recollection like the one above describing your repeated reading, viewing, or listening.

_____

_____

_____

_____

**G.** Pick any two countries. Search online or in an encyclopedia to find out which country is bigger, which has a larger population (xxx 的人比 xxx 的人多), which country's summer is hotter, which country's winter is colder, which country's spring or fall is more pleasant, etc. Write a paragraph comparing the two countries. (PRESENTATIONAL)

# H. Storytelling (PRESENTATIONAL)

Write a story in Chinese based on the four cartoons below. Make sure that your story has a beginning, middle, and end. Also make sure that the transition from one picture to the next is smooth and logical.

**1**
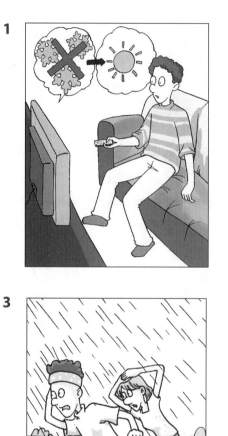

**2**

**3**

**4**

| 城市 | 天气 | 最高气温 | 最低气温 | 城市 | 天气 | 最高气温 | 最低气温 |
|------|------|----------|----------|------|------|----------|----------|
| 北京 | | 31 | 22 | 石家庄 | | 31 | 22 |
| 哈尔滨 | | 27 | 18 | 济南 | | 30 | 22 |
| 长春 | | 27 | 19 | 郑州 | | 28 | 20 |
| 沈阳 | | 28 | 20 | 合肥 | | 29 | 24 |
| 天津 | | 31 | 22 | 南京 | | 29 | 24 |
| 呼和浩特 | | 27 | 16 | 上海 | | 35 | 27 |
| 乌鲁木齐 | | 37 | 23 | 武汉 | | 30 | 23 |
| 西宁 | | 24 | 12 | 长沙 | | 33 | 24 |
| 银川 | | 29 | 19 | 南昌 | | 30 | 25 |
| 兰州 | | 31 | 19 | 杭州 | | 35 | 25 |
| 西安 | | 35 | 23 | 福州 | | 36 | 27 |
| 拉萨 | | 20 | 9 | 南宁 | | 33 | 25 |
| 成都 | | 32 | 24 | 海口 | | 34 | 26 |
| 重庆 | | 35 | 25 | 广州 | | 33 | 26 |

中国城市的天气预报

**LESSON 12** **Dining**
第十二课 吃饭

**PART ONE** **Dialogue I: Dining Out**

## I. Listening Comprehension

**A. Textbook Dialogue** (Multiple Choice) (INTERPRETIVE)

Indicate the correct answer in the parentheses.

( ) **1.** **a.** Wang Peng and Li You did not have to wait to be seated.

  **b.** Wang Peng and Li You had to wait a long time for a table.

  **c.** The restaurant was not crowded at all.

  **d.** There was still a table available.

( ) **2.** **a.** Wang Peng and Li You ordered food separately.

  **b.** Li You asked Wang Peng to order for her.

  **c.** Wang Peng offered to order for Li You.

  **d.** Wang Peng did not want to order for Li You.

( ) **3.** **a.** The diners ordered two dishes plus soup.

  **b.** Wang Peng ordered three dishes and a soup.

  **c.** Li You did not order any soup.

  **d.** Wang Peng ordered two different soups for himself and Li You.

( ) **4.** **a.** Wang Peng did not want any ice in his beverage.

  **b.** Wang Peng asked for lots of ice in his beverage.

  **c.** Li You asked for lots of ice in her beverage.

  **d.** Wang Peng and Li You both wanted lots of ice in their beverages.

( ) **5. a.** Both Wang Peng and Li You are vegetarians.

   **b.** Li You is a vegetarian.

   **c.** Wang Peng prefers vegetarian dumplings.

   **d.** Li You occasionally eats meat.

## B. Workbook Dialogue (True/False) (INTERPRETIVE)

( ) **1.** The man and the woman are at home.

( ) **2.** The woman has completely changed her diet.

( ) **3.** The woman suggests meat dumplings because she does not want to be difficult.

( ) **4.** The woman still doesn't eat meat at home.

( ) **5.** The man suggests vegetable dumplings because the woman is a vegetarian.

## C. Listening Rejoinder (INTERPERSONAL)

In this section, you will hear two speakers talking. After hearing the first speaker, select the best from the four possible responses given by the second speaker.

---

# II. Speaking Exercises

**A.** Answer the questions in Chinese based on the Textbook Dialogue. (INTERPRETIVE/PRESENTATIONAL)

   **1.** What was Li You's impression when she entered the restaurant?

   **2.** Was there meat in the dumplings or the tofu dish that Li You and Wang Peng ordered? Why or why not?

   **3.** What special requests did Li You make for her hot and sour soup?

   **4.** Did Li You and Wang Peng have any vegetable dishes? Why or why not?

   **5.** What drinks did Li You and Wang Peng order?

**B.** Ask your partner what kinds of drinks he/she usually orders in a restaurant. (INTERPERSONAL)

**C.** With a partner, participate in a simulated conversation in a restaurant. One of you will be a customer and the other the waiter/waitress. The customer will order a main dish, a soup, and a drink and give special requests about the dish or the drink. The waiter/waitress recommends a dish, politely takes the order, and repeats what the customer wants at the end. (INTERPERSONAL)

# III. Reading Comprehension (INTERPRETIVE)

## A. Building Words

If you combine the *shū* in *kàn shū* with the *zhuō* in *zhuōzi*, you have *shūzhuō*, as seen in #1 below. Can you guess what the word *shūzhuō* means? Complete this section by providing the characters, the *pinyin* and the English equivalent of each new word formed this way. You may consult a dictionary if necessary.

|  |  | new word | *pinyin* | English |
|---|---|---|---|---|
| **1.** | "看书"的"书" + "桌子"的"桌"<br>→  书+桌  → | _____ | _____ | _____ |
| **2.** | "吃饭"的"饭" + "桌子"的"桌"<br>→  饭+桌  → | _____ | _____ | _____ |
| **3.** | "青菜"的"菜" + "刀"<br>→  菜+刀  → | _____ | _____ | _____ |
| **4.** | "吃素"的"素" + "点菜"的"菜"<br>→  素+菜  → | _____ | _____ | _____ |
| **5.** | "喝茶"的"茶" + "饭馆"的"馆"<br>→  茶+馆  → | _____ | _____ | _____ |

**B.** Read the dialogue below and answer the questions.

李小姐：服务员，你们的家常豆腐一点儿也不好吃。酸辣汤也很糟糕。我点菜的时候告诉你我不喜欢味精，可是好像还是放了很多味精。

服务员：对不起，小姐，可是菜你都吃完了。大家都说我们饭馆儿的菜很不错，有的菜六点钟就卖完了。

李小姐：你自己觉得这儿的菜怎么样？

服务员：我不知道。

李小姐：你怎么不知道？你在这儿工作，不在这儿吃饭
　　　　吗？

服务员：我真的不知道，因为我和别的服务员都去别的
　　　　饭馆儿吃饭。

Questions (Multiple Choice)

(  ) **1.** Miss Li did not like the soup because _____.

     **a.** it was too hot

     **b.** it was too sour

     **c.** it was not cooked in the way she wanted

(  ) **2.** What does the waiter suggest in his comment on the food?

     **a.** Since Miss Li finished the food, it must have been okay.

     **b.** Miss Li finished it even though it was not good.

     **c.** Because it was good, it had sold out.

(  ) **3.** The waiter tried to defend his restaurant by saying that _____.

     **a.** some of its dishes often sold out very quickly

     **b.** some customers had to come early

     **c.** some dishes had to be cooked early

(  ) **4.** Miss Li assumed that _____.

     **a.** the waiter did not have his meals in the restaurant, even though he worked there

     **b.** the waiter had his daily lunch in the restaurant since he worked there

     **c.** the waiter had his lunch in the restaurant when he did not work there

(  ) **5.** How did the waiter like the food in his restaurant?

     **a.** He didn't like it, even though he ate it every day.

     **b.** He liked it, but was not allowed to eat there.

     **c.** He didn't know since he had never eaten at the restaurant.

**C.** Read the passage and answer the questions.

　　王朋和李友昨天晚上六点钟到一家饭馆儿吃饭。他们要了两杯可乐。王朋点了一盘肉和一盘饺子。李友一点儿肉也不吃，所以只要了一盘豆腐。两杯可乐很快就来了，可是到了七点半一盘菜都没上。王朋问服务员："我们的菜做好了吗？"服务员说："你们现在饿了吗？"王朋和李友都说："我们都饿了。"服务员告诉他们："我们饭馆儿跟别的饭馆儿不一样。要是你不太饿，你会觉得我们的菜一点儿也不好吃。要是你真饿了，才会觉得我们的菜特别好吃。所以我得等你们很饿了才上菜。"

Questions (True/False)

(　) **1.** Li You ordered a Coke and a vegetarian dish.

(　) **2.** Wang Peng and Li You waited for their drinks for a long time.

(　) **3.** At 7:30, there was still one dish that had not yet arrived.

(　) **4.** We can assume that Wang Peng and Li You will visit this restaurant again soon.

Questions (Multiple Choice)

(　) **5.** According to the waiter, this restaurant is different from others because ____.

　　**a.** its tasty food makes customers feel even hungrier

　　**b.** its customers can never have enough of its delicious food

　　**c.** its food is tasty only to hungry customers

(　) **6.** According to the waiter, he had to ____.

　　**a.** wait for Wang Peng and Li You to become really hungry

　　**b.** wait on other hungry customers first

　　**c.** eat first because he was hungry

**D.**

No0032733 **价 目 表**

| 品　　　　名 | 单价 | 数　　　量 | 金额 |
|---|---|---|---|
| 招 牌 锅 贴 | 4 | | |
| 韭 菜 锅 贴 | 4 | | |
| 辣 味 锅 贴 | 5 | | |
| 招 牌 水 饺 | 5 | | |
| 韭 菜 水 饺 | 5 | | |
| 辣 味 水 饺 | 5 | | |
| 素　　　水 饺 | 5 | | |
| 鲜 虾 水 饺 | 7 | | |
| **汤 类** | | | |
| 酸 辣 汤 | 25 | | |
| 玉 米 浓 汤 | 25 | | |
| 旗 鱼 丸 汤 | 25 | | |
| 原 汁 豆 浆 | 15 | | |
| 纯 黑 豆 浆 | 15 | | |
| 米　　　　浆 | 15 | | |
| 小　　　　菜 | | | |
| | | | |

合计 :＿＿＿＿＿＿＿

**1.** What can you order from this menu if you are a vegetarian?

**2.** How much is their hot and sour soup?

# IV. Writing Exercises

**A.** Give the appropriate number, measure word, and noun for each picture. Each measure word can only be used once.

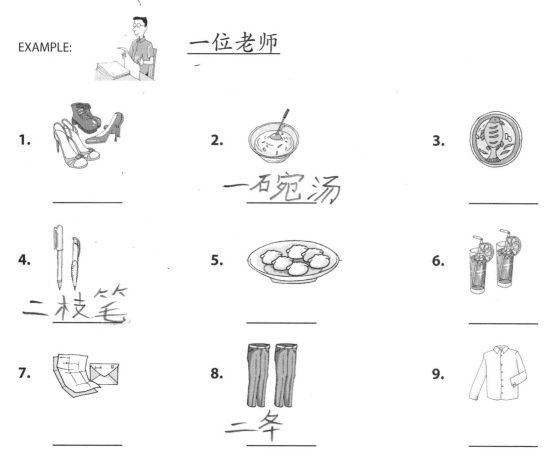

EXAMPLE: 一位老师

1. _____

2. 一石宛汤
   _____

3. _____

4. 二枝笔
   _____

5. _____

6. _____

7. _____

8. 二条
   _____

9. _____

**B.** This past winter break, Little Gao was too busy to do anything and had too little money to buy anything.

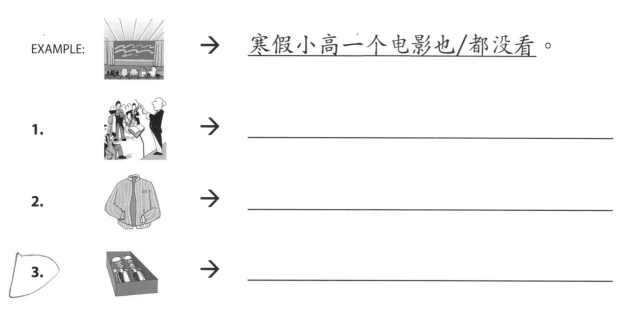

EXAMPLE: → 寒假小高一个电影也/都没看。

1. → _____

2. → _____

3. → _____

**C.** Mr. Li is not feeling well and doesn't have an appetite for anything.

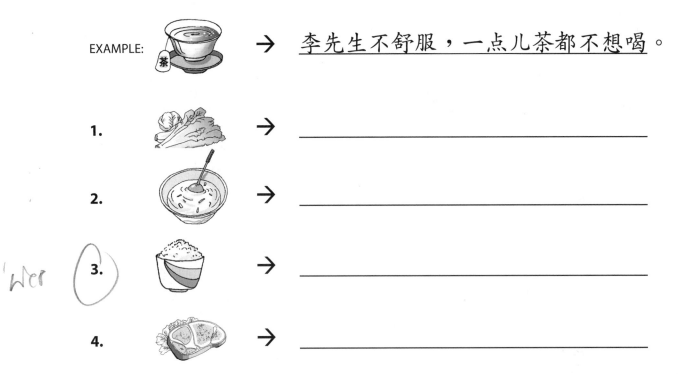

EXAMPLE: → <u>李先生不舒服，一点儿茶都不想喝</u>。

1. → _____

2. → _____

*Wei* (3.) → _____

4. → _____

**D.** Imagine that you're evaluating your own academic progress. If you wish to do better in school, what advice would you give yourself? What should you do more? What should you do less?

多···                          少···

_____        _____

_____        _____

_____        _____

_____        _____

···                          ···

## E. In Other Words

Little Wang always listens to his mother. If his mother says: "要是功课没做好，就不能玩儿，" he knows it means, in other words, "功课做好了，才能玩儿。" Let's see what other parental directions Little Wang listens to.

**1.** 要是饭没吃完，就不能玩儿。

In other words: _____

**2.** 要是汉字没写对，就不能玩儿。

In other words: _____

**3.** 要是录音没听懂，就不能玩儿。

In other words: _____

**4.** 要是考试没准备好，就不能玩儿。

In other words: _____

**F.** Translate the following into Chinese. (PRESENTATIONAL)

**1.** **A:** Do you use MSG when you cook?

_____

**B:** No, I don't. Not even a bit.

_____

**2.** **A:** Eat some more. Aren't you hungry?

_____

**B:** I am hungry. But I am a vegetarian.

_____

**A:** Is that right? I'll make some vegetable dumplings. They will be ready in no time.

_____

**B:** Thank you.

_____

这些是豆腐。

## PART TWO    Dialogue II: Eating in a Cafeteria

### I. Listening Comprehension

**A. Textbook Dialogue** (True/False) (INTERPRETIVE)

( )  **1.**  There was nothing good to eat in the student cafeteria.

( )  **2.**  The sweet and sour fish was very tasty.

( )  **3.**  Wang Peng didn't like the chef's recommendation.

( )  **4.**  Wang Peng didn't have any cash on him.

( )  **5.**  The chef shortchanged Wang Peng.

**B. Workbook Dialogue** (Multiple Choice) (INTERPRETIVE)

( )  **1.**  Who will cook tonight?

   **a.**  The woman will do all the cooking tonight.
   **b.**  The woman will do most of the cooking tonight.
   **c.**  The man will do all the cooking tonight.
   **d.**  The man will do most of the cooking tonight.

( )  **2.**  Who wants soup?

   **a.**  the man
   **b.**  the woman
   **c.**  both the man and the woman
   **d.**  neither the man nor the woman

( )  **3.**  Which of the following statements is true?

   **a.**  The man will make the soup.
   **b.**  The woman will make the soup.
   **c.**  The man and the woman will make the soup together.
   **d.**  The man and the woman will each make their own soup.

( )  **4.**  The woman offers to make the soup because _____.

   **a.**  the man doesn't know how to make it
   **b.**  she doesn't like how the man makes it
   **c.**  she wants to help
   **d.**  the man doesn't feel like making soup

## C. Listening Rejoinder (INTERPERSONAL)

In this section, you will hear two speakers talking. After hearing the first speaker, select the best from the four possible responses given by the second speaker.

_____

# II. Speaking Exercises

**A.** Answer the questions in Chinese based on the Textbook Dialogue. (INTERPRETIVE/PRESENTATIONAL)

1. How did the chef describe the fish in sweet and sour sauce?
2. Did Wang Peng order the beef braised in soy sauce?
3. What did Wang Peng finally order?
4. What was the amount of change that the chef gave to Wang Peng and why?

**B.** Ask your friend how much he/she usually spends on lunch. (INTERPERSONAL)

**C.** With a partner, participate in a simulated conversation. You ask your partner (a waiter in a restaurant) the total cost of your order. He/she tells you the price and you pay with an approximate amount of cash. He/she gives you the wrong amount of change, either more or less than what should be given. Politely explain to him/her how the amount of change is wrong. (INTERPERSONAL)

# III. Reading Comprehension

## A. Building Words

If you combine the *mǐ* in *mǐfàn* with the *cù* in *tángcùyú*, you have *mǐcù*, as seen in #1 below. Can you guess what the word *mǐcù* means? Complete this section by providing the characters, the *pinyin* and the English equivalent of each new word formed this way. You may consult a dictionary if necessary.

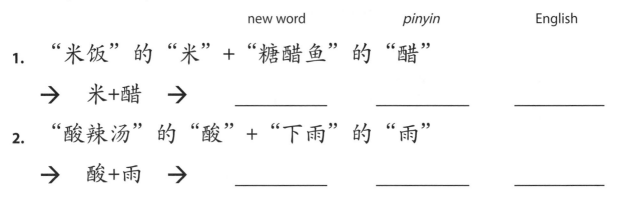

|  | new word | *pinyin* | English |
|---|---|---|---|
| 1. "米饭"的"米"+"糖醋鱼"的"醋" → 米+醋 → | _____ | _____ | _____ |
| 2. "酸辣汤"的"酸"+"下雨"的"雨" → 酸+雨 → | _____ | _____ | _____ |

3.  "金" + "糖醋鱼" 的 "鱼"

    →    金+鱼    →    _____    _____    _____

4.  "凉拌" 的 "凉" + "鞋"

    →    凉+鞋    →    _____    _____    _____

5.  "喝水" 的 "水" + "牛肉" 的 "牛"

    →    水+牛    →    _____    _____    _____

**B.** Read the dialogue and answer the questions. (INTERPRETIVE)

李先生：请问，你们的红烧牛肉怎么样？

服务员：好吃极了。

李先生：你们的家常豆腐好不好？

服务员：家常豆腐比红烧牛肉更好吃。

李先生：那你们的糖醋鱼呢？

服务员：糖醋鱼比家常豆腐更好吃。

李先生：你们的菜都好吃，那我点什么呢？还是给我一盘
　　　　红烧牛肉吧。

服务员：好，红烧牛肉比糖醋鱼更好吃。

李先生：你刚才说家常豆腐比红烧牛肉更好吃。算了吧，
　　　　我不点菜了。我去别的饭馆吧。

服务员：先生，为什么？

李先生：因为你不知道哪个菜好吃。

Questions (True/False)

( )**1.** Mr. Li was very familiar with the menu.

( )**2.** The waiter believed that beef in soy sauce was the most delicious dish on the
menu.

(　) **3.** Mr. Li was most likely a vegetarian.

(　) **4.** In the end, Mr. Li did not eat at this restaurant.

Questions (Multiple Choice)

(　) **5.** Which of the following statements is true?

    **a.** The waiter was genuinely enthusiastic about the food in his restaurant.

    **b.** The waiter tried to familiarize Mr. Li with the menu.

    **c.** The waiter tried to push Mr. Li for a quick order.

(　) **6.** Mr. Li decided to eat elsewhere because

    **a.** he was overwhelmed by all the choices at the restaurant.

    **b.** he lost count of the number of dishes.

    **c.** he realized that the service there was too slow.

**C.** Answer the questions based on the reading passage.

　　小谢和小张刚打完球，现在又饿又渴。他们走进一家餐厅，想点些吃的和喝的东西。可是他们两个人一共只有三十二块五毛钱。他们最少得点一个素菜，一个荤菜（hūncài, 有肉的菜），一碗汤，两碗饭，两个人还得喝点东西。不过小谢不吃辣的菜，小张不能喝茶或者咖啡。要是你是小谢或者小张，你怎么办？下边是餐厅的菜单，请你看一下，然后告诉师傅你们想吃什么，喝什么。

菜单

| | | |
|---|---|---|
| 素饺子 | 6.25 | （一盘） |
| 牛肉饺子 | 6.75 | （一盘） |
| 红烧牛肉 | 7.95 | |
| 糖醋牛肉 | 7.75 | |
| 红烧鱼 | 8.75 | |
| 糖醋鱼 | 8.75 | |
| *家常豆腐 | 6.50 | |
| 红烧豆腐 | 6.50 | |
| *凉拌黄瓜 | 6.25 | |
| 白菜豆腐汤 | 3.75 | （两人份） |
| 白饭 | 0.75 | |
| 可乐 | 1.50 | |
| 绿茶 | 1.25 | |
| 红茶 | 1.25 | |
| 咖啡 | 1.25 | |

*＝辣的菜

看了菜单以后，现在请你帮小谢和小张点菜。

点菜单

第一道菜：_____  $_____

第二道菜：_____  $_____

第三道菜：_____  $_____

汤：_____  $_____

喝的东西：_____  $_____

饭：_____  $_____

$_____

**D.** Read the passage below. Then answer the first two questions in English, and the third in Chinese. (INTERPRETIVE/PRESENTATIONAL)

小夏渴极了，也饿极了。他走进饭馆，想点一杯凉凉的、甜甜的可乐。可是，上个星期医生告诉他得少喝甜的东西。他又想点茶或者咖啡，也不行，因为喝了会让他紧张。那来碗酸辣汤吧！可是医生说他一点儿辣的都不能吃。算了，算了，多喝水吧！小夏想点牛肉，不过，最近牛肉好像有问题。那还是吃鱼吧！可是服务员告诉他鱼卖完了。糟糕！那吃什么呢？最后，小夏点了一盘素饺子，一盘豆腐，一盘凉拌黄瓜。吃完以后，小夏觉得不够，还觉得饿。要是你是小夏，这个时候你怎么办？

1. List on the left all the drinks and the dishes that Little Xia wished to order but didn't, and explain on the right why he didn't.

_____    _____

_____    _____

_____    _____

_____    _____

_____    _____

2. What did Little Xia end up having at the restaurant? Do you like his choices? Why or why not?

_____

3. Answer the question at the end of the story.

_____

**E.** Look at the prices displayed and answer the following question.

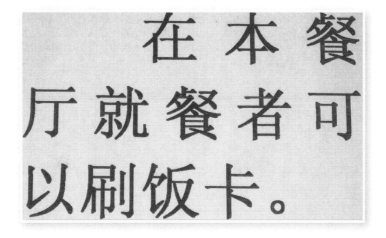

How much is the cucumber salad? _____


**F.** Read the notice posted and answer the following question.

在 本 餐
厅 就 餐 者 可
以 刷 饭 卡。

Can one use meal cards in this particular cafeteria? _____

# IV. Writing Exercises

## A. Building Characters

Form a character by fitting the given components together as indicated. Then provide a word, a phrase, or a short sentence in which that character appears.

EXAMPLE: a 口 on the left with a 加 as in 加州 : It is the character <u>咖</u> as in <u>咖啡</u>.

1.  a 口 on the top with a 贝 at the bottom: It is the character _____ as

    in _____ .

2.  a 米 as in 米饭 on the left with a 青 as in 青菜 on the right: It is the character

    _____ as in _____ .

3.  a side 亻 radical on the left with a 我 on the right: It is the character _____ as

    in _____ .

4.  a three-dot water radical on the left with a 青 as in 青菜 on the right: It is the

    character _____ as in _____ .

5.  a three-dot water on the left with a 每 as in 每天 on the right: It is the character

    _____ as in _____ .

**B.** Everyone's palate and dietary restrictions are different. According to your own preferences, what will you say to the waiter when you order dishes? 多放 (duō fàng)…or 少放 (shǎo fàng)…

(PRESENTATIONAL)

...                                              ...

**C.** Place your order based on the illustrations given. (PRESENTATIONAL)

EXAMPLE:    →    <u>服务员，来两碗米饭</u>。

1.    →    _____ 。

2.    →    _____ 。

3.    →    _____ 。

4.    →    _____ 。

**D.** What First Comes to Mind: When hearing 酸辣汤, many people who like that soup will immediately think of the expression 酸酸的、辣辣的，很好喝. How about the following? (INTERPRETIVE/PRESENTATIONAL)

1. 糖醋鱼：_____

2. 凉拌豆腐：_____

3. 冰咖啡：_____

**E.** Answer the following questions based on your own situation. (INTERPERSONAL)

1. **A:** 你觉得中国菜好吃还是美国菜好吃？

   **B:** _____

2. **A:** 你喜欢吃青菜还是吃肉？

   **B:** _____

3. **A:** 天气热的时候，你喜欢喝什么？

   **B:** _____

4. **A:** 你平常先喝汤再吃饭，还是先吃饭再喝汤？

   **B:** _____

5. **A:** 你能吃辣的吗？

   **B:** _____

6. **A:** 要是你不能吃味精，你跟服务员说什么？

   **B:** _____

**F.** Translate the following into Chinese. (PRESENTATIONAL)

1. **A:** We just finished our exam. I asked Xiao Li to have dinner with us tomorrow.

   _____

   **B:** Great! What should we make then?

   _____

   **A:** He likes to eat meat. We'll make beef in soy sauce, and sweet and sour fish. How's that?

   _____

   **B:** You are a vegetarian. I'll make some vegetarian dumplings and a cucumber salad.

   _____

   **A:** Good. Xiao Li likes vegetarian dumplings and cucumber salad, too.

   _____

**2.** Yesterday was Little Wang's birthday. I treated him to dinner. We went to a Chinese restaurant. When we got there, there wasn't even a single customer. The waiter asked us what we would like to eat. I ordered a plate of dumplings. Little Wang said he was hungry and thirsty. He ordered a Coke, a tofu dish, and a sweet and sour fish. The waiter wanted us to order one more dish. We said we'd already ordered enough food. But the dumplings were all sold out and the fish was too sour. The waiter not only served the food slowly, but also gave the wrong change. The service there was really terrible. We'd better not go there any more in the future.

## G. Today's Special (PRESENTATIONAL)

Pretend that you're a restaurant manager. Make a flier to promote your specials of the day. The flier has to include one spicy dish, one meat dish, one vegetable dish, and one soup. Make sure to include wording that promotes your dishes on the flier, and don't forget to mention that you don't put any MSG in your dishes.

## H. Storytelling (PRESENTATIONAL)

Write a story based on the four cartoons below. Make sure that your story has a beginning, middle and end. Also make sure that the transition from one picture to the next is smooth and logical.

# LESSON 13    Asking Directions
## 第十三课 问路

13

---

**PART ONE**    **Dialogue I: Where Are You Off To?**

## 🔘 I. Listening Comprehension

### A. Textbook Dialogue (Multiple Choice) (INTERPRETIVE)

( ) **1.** Chang Laoshi asks Bai Ying'ai where she is going because

    **a.** Chang Laoshi is nosy.

    **b.** this is a common greeting.

    **c.** Chang Laoshi needs to know where Little Bai is going.

    **d.** Bai Ying'ai looks lost.

( ) **2.** Does Bai Ying'ai know how to get to the computer center?

    **a.** No, Bai Ying'ai doesn't know how to get to the computer center.

    **b.** No, Bai Ying'ai has forgotten how to get to the computer center.

    **c.** No, Bai Ying'ai has no idea where the computer center is.

    **d.** No, and Chang Laoshi doesn't know how to get to the computer center, either.

( ) **3.** Which description of the campus is correct?

    **a.** The library is between the computer center and the student activity center.

    **b.** The student activity center is between the library and the computer center.

    **c.** The computer center is between the library and the student activity center.

    **d.** The computer center is between Wang Peng's dorm and the library.

( ) **4.** Chang Laoshi and Bai Ying'ai will walk together because

    **a.** Chang Laoshi enjoys Bai Ying'ai's company.

    **b.** Chang Laoshi's destination is not far away from Bai Ying'ai's.

    **c.** Bai Ying'ai asks Chang Laoshi to.

    **d.** they haven't seen each other for a long time.

### B. Workbook Dialogue (True/False) (INTERPRETIVE)

( ) The woman doesn't know where the athletic field is.

( ) The man doesn't know where the computer center is.

( ) The woman is on her way to the computer center.

( ) The athletic field is between the library and the computer center.

### C. Listening Rejoinder (INTERPERSONAL)

In this section, you will hear two speakers talking. After hearing the first speaker, select the best from the four possible responses given by the second speaker.

_____

# II. Speaking Exercises

**A.** Answer the questions in Chinese based on the Textbook Dialogue. (INTERPRETIVE/PRESENTATIONAL)

**1.** Where did Bai Ying'ai want to go?

**2.** Which place is farther from the classroom, the computer center or the athletic field?

**3.** Where is the computer center?

**4.** Why did Teacher Chang suggest that Bai Ying'ai and she should go together?

**B.** Draw a simple map of your school's campus and indicate the locations of the library, student activity center, your Chinese classroom, the computer center, and the athletic field in relation to each other. With a partner, do a role play. Pretend you are a new student and ask your partner where the school library and the student activity center are. (INTERPERSONAL)

# III. Reading Comprehension (INTERPRETIVE)

### A. Building Words

If you combine the *jìn* in *yuǎnjìn* with the *lù* in *gāosù gōnglù*, you have *jìnlù*, as seen in #1 below. Can you guess what the word *jìnlù* means? Complete this section by providing the characters, the *pinyin*, and the English equivalent of each new word formed this way. You may consult a dictionary if necessary.

|  | | new word | *pinyin* | English |
|---|---|---|---|---|
| **1.** | "远近" 的 "近" + "高速公路" 的 "路" → 近+路 → | _____ | _____ | _____ |
| **2.** | "运动" 的 "动" + "生词" 的 "词" → 动+词 → | _____ | _____ | _____ |

3. "远近"的"远"+"电视"的"视"

   →   远+视  →   _____   _____   _____

4. "远近"的"近"+"电视"的"视"

   →   近+视  →   _____   _____   _____

5. "书店"的"店"+"服务员"的"员"

   →   店+员  →   _____   _____   _____

**B.** Read the following passage and answer the questions.

小钱的家离学校很远。每天早上，他都得先坐公共汽车，然后坐地铁，才能到学校。因为每天去学校上课都得花很多时间，所以他觉得很累，希望能换一个学校。他希望新学校离家近一点儿。

Questions: (True/False)

( ) **1.** Little Qian lives in a student dorm.
( ) **2.** Little Qian's home is on the subway line.
( ) **3.** The destination of his bus ride is the subway station.
( ) **4.** Little Qian doesn't mind the commute.
( ) **5.** If he could, Little Qian would like to go to a different school.

**C.** Read the following passage and answer the questions.

蓝先生早上想到学校运动场去运动，可是他不知道运动场在哪儿。八点钟，他在图书馆前边看到李友，问李友运动场在哪儿，比书店近还是比书店远？李友告诉他运动场没有书店那么远。蓝先生走到了书店，可是没有看到运动场。书店的售货员告诉他，运动场就在电脑中心的旁边。蓝先生到了电脑中心，也没找到运动场，因为他不知道学校有两个书店和两个电脑中心。九点钟蓝先生又回到了图书馆。李友问:"您去运动场运动了吗?"蓝先生说:"不运动了,我今天已经走够了。"

Questions (True/False)

( )  **1.** Mr. Lan does not know the campus well.

( )  **2.** Mr. Lan went to the library with Li You.

( )  **3.** According to Li You, Mr. Lan should see the athletic field before the bookstore.

( )  **4.** It is likely that Li You was in the library for at least an hour.

( )  **5.** In the end, Mr. Lan didn't want to go to the athletic field anymore because he had enough exercise already trying to find it.

( )  **6.** Mr. Lan didn't find the athletic field because of a miscommunication.

**D.** Look at the map and answer the question.

第一教学楼离图书馆近还是第二教学楼离图书馆近?

_____

# IV. Writing Exercises

**A.** For each pair of pictures, write two sentences describing Little Gao's opinions.

EXAMPLE:    ✓    ✗    delicious

→ <u>小高觉得饺子比米饭好吃。</u>

<u>小高觉得米饭没有饺子好吃。</u>

1.    ✓ 中文    ✗ English    difficult

→ _____

_____

2.    ✓    ✗    fun/interesting

→ _____

_____

3.    ✓    ✗ cola    expensive

→ _____

_____

**B.** List the activities that students can do at the student center at your school.

EXAMPLE: 学生可以到学生活动中心去运动。

1. _____

2. _____

3. _____

4. _____

5. _____

...

**C.** Imagine that you are a campus planner. Draw a plan of an ideal school. Where would you situate the library, classrooms, dorms, teachers' office building, computer center, and athletic facilities in relation to one another? Explain why in Chinese. (PRESENTATIONAL)

_____

_____

_____

**D.** Translate the following into Chinese. (PRESENTATIONAL)

**1.  A:**  Is the bookstore between the student center and the athletic field?

_____

   **B:**  No, it's inside that dorm.

_____

**2.  A:**  I heard the park isn't far away from here. Do you know how to get there?

_____

   **B:**  Yes, I do. I'm heading there, too. Let's go together.

_____

   **A:**  Great!

_____

## PART TWO    Dialogue II: Going to Chinatown

## I. Listening Comprehension

### A. Textbook Dialogue (Multiple Choice) (INTERPRETIVE)

( ) **1.** Who has been to Chinatown before?

    **a.** Both Wang Peng and Gao Wenzhong have been to Chinatown many times.

    **b.** Wang Peng has been to Chinatown before.

    **c.** Neither Gao Wenzhong nor Wang Peng has been to Chinatown before.

    **d.** Gao Wenzhong has been to Chinatown before.

( ) **2.** Do they have a map?

    **a.** Wang Peng has a map in his car.

    **b.** Gao Wenzhong brought a map.

    **c.** Gao Wenzhong forgot to bring a map.

    **d.** Wang Peng doesn't need a map.

( ) **3.** Where do they end up?

    **a.** in Chinatown

    **b.** back at Wang Peng's place

    **c.** at a traffic light

    **d.** in Little Tokyo

### B. Workbook Dialogue (Multiple Choice) (INTERPRETIVE)

( ) **1.** Where did the speakers think they were heading?

    **a.** a restaurant in Beijing

    **b.** a restaurant in Tokyo

    **c.** a restaurant called Beijing

    **d.** a restaurant called Tokyo

( ) **2.** The woman worried that they might not be able to get a seat in the restaurant because

    **a.** it would take another six blocks to get to the restaurant.

    **b.** it was Friday and a lot of people were dining out.

    **c.** the restaurant didn't take reservations.

    **d.** no one answered the phone at the restaurant.

( ) **3.** They end up having Japanese food because

    **a.** they had Chinese food last weekend.

    **b.** they are going to Tokyo soon.

    **c.** the man called the wrong restaurant.

    **d.** the Japanese restaurant is closer.

## C. Listening Rejoinder (INTERPERSONAL)

In this section, you will hear two speakers talking. After hearing the first speaker, select the best from the four possible responses given by the second speaker.

_____

# II. Speaking Exercises

**A.** Answer the questions in Chinese based on the Textbook Dialogue. (INTERPRETIVE/PRESENTATIONAL)

    **1.** Why didn't Wang Peng know where Chinatown was?

    **2.** Did Wang Peng and Gao Wenzhong have a map with them? Why or why not?

    **3.** What directions did Gao Wenzhong give Wang Peng to get to Chinatown?

    **4.** Why didn't they make a turn at the fourth intersection?

    **5.** Did Wang Peng and Gao Wenzhong arrive in Chinatown? Why or why not?

**B.** Ask your partner if he/she has ever been to a Chinatown. If so, ask what he/she did there. If not, ask how he/she would like to spend a day in Chinatown. (INTERPERSONAL)

**C.** Tell your classmates how to get to your place from school. Draw a map to illustrate the route. (PRESENTATIONAL)

# III. Reading Comprehension (INTERPRETIVE)

## A. Building Words

If you combine the *zuǒ* in *zuǒbian* with *shǒu*, you have *zuǒshǒu*, as seen in #1 below. Can you guess what the word *zuǒshǒu* means? Complete this section by providing the characters, the *pinyin*, and the English equivalent of each new word formed this way. You may consult a dictionary if necessary.

|  | new word | *pinyin* | English |
|---|---|---|---|

1.  "左边" 的 "左" + "手"

    → 左+手 → _____   _____   _____

2.  "右边" 的 "右" + "手"

    → 右+手 → _____   _____   _____

3.  "前面" 的 "前" + "门"

    → 前+门 → _____   _____   _____

4.  "红绿灯" 的 "红" + "冰茶" 的 "茶"

    → 红+茶 → _____   _____   _____

5.  "红绿灯" 的 "绿" + "冰茶" 的 "茶"

    → 绿+茶 → _____   _____   _____

**B.** Answer the following questions according to the map of the campus.

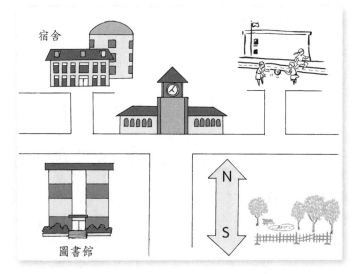

Questions: (True/False)

( ) 1. 学生宿舍的东边有一个公园。

( ) 2. 图书馆在学生宿舍的南边。

( ) 3. 学生宿舍在运动场的西边。

( ) 4. 公园的北边有公共汽车站。

**C.** Read the following passage and answer the questions.

老李去过中国城买东西、吃中国饭，但是每次都是坐朋友的车去。上个周末老李自己开车到中国城去，车里没有地图，他走错了。他想回家去拿地图，可是找不到回家的路。他想问问朋友，可是没有手机。老李很紧张，就到旁边的饭馆儿问。饭馆儿的师傅告诉他一直往东开，过三个红绿灯就能看到中国城了。

1. What had Old Li done in Chinatown in the past?
2. How did he go to Chinatown in the past?
3. Why couldn't he locate Chinatown last weekend?
4. Why didn't he go home for a map?
5. Why didn't he call someone for help?
6. Who gave him directions?
7. How did he finally find Chinatown?

**D.** Read the following passage and answer the questions.

快考试了，我得去书店买书复习复习，但我没去过书店。小白说走到那里太慢，开车很快就能到。她说从学校出来，先上大学路，一直往南开，到第一个红绿灯往东开。然后到了第一个路口往左一拐就会看到路的右边有一家活动中心。再往前走，过一个中国饭馆就会看到路的左边有一家鞋店，书店就在鞋店的旁边。

1.  What did the narrator want to buy? Why was she so anxious?

    _____

2.  According to Little Bai, which way was more convenient to go to the narrator's destination, driving or walking?

    _____

3.  Based on Little Bai's directions, draw a map of the route to the narrator's destination and indicate all the landmarks.

    _____

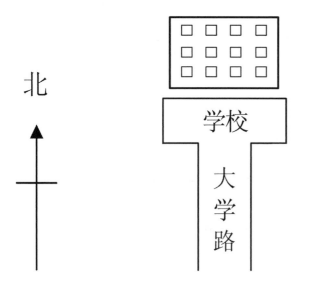

**E.** Look at the map and answer the question in Chinese.

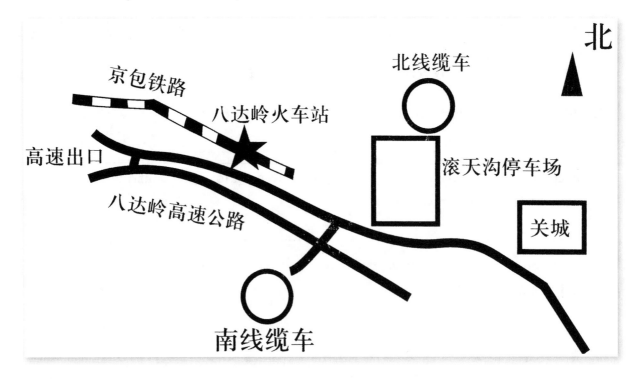

Is the train station to the north, east, south, or west of the highway?_____

# IV. Writing Exercises

## A. Building Characters

Form a character by fitting the given components together as indicated. Then provide a word or phrase in which that character appears.

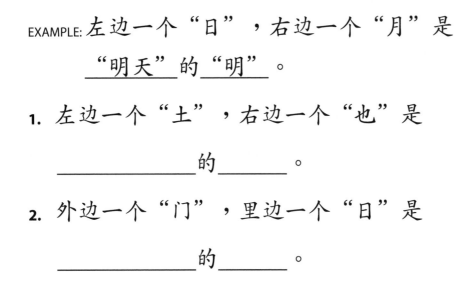

EXAMPLE: 左边一个"日"，右边一个"月"是

　　"明天"的"明"。

1. 左边一个"土"，右边一个"也"是

　　_____的_____。

2. 外边一个"门"，里边一个"日"是

　　_____的_____。

3. 上边一个"合适"的"合"，下边一个"手"是

_____的_____。

4. 上边一个"山"，下边一个"山"是

_____的_____。

5. 上边一个"口"，下边一个"八"是

_____的_____。

**B.** Ask and answer the following questions based on your own experience.

EXAMPLE: cucumber salad

A: 你吃过凉拌黄瓜吗？　　　　B: 我吃过。

A: 你觉得凉拌黄瓜好吃吗？　　B: 我觉得凉拌黄瓜

　　　　　　　　　　　　　　　　很好吃/不好吃。

or

A: 你吃过凉拌黄瓜吗？　　　　B: 我没吃过。

A: 你想吃吗？　　　　　　　　B: 我想吃/我不想吃。

1. family style tofu

_____　　_____

2. sweet and sour fish

_____　　_____

**3.** hot and sour soup

_____          _____

**4.** vegetable dumplings

_____          _____

**5.** baby bok choy

_____          _____


**C.** Using the table as a reference point, ask and answer where each item is located.

**1.**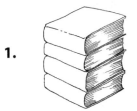

_____

**2.**

_____

**3.**

_____

**4.**

_____

**D.** Locate the buildings based on the map.

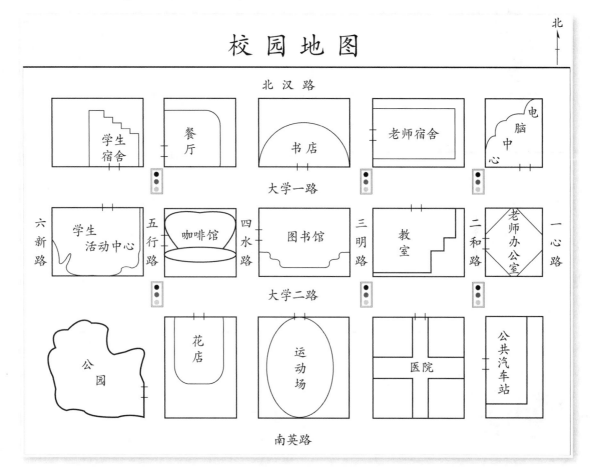

EXAMPLE: bookstore

A: 书店在哪儿？　　　B: 书店在餐厅的东边。/

书店在老师宿舍的西边。/

书店在餐厅和老师宿舍的中间…

1. student activity center _____

2. teachers' offices _____

3. coffee shop _____

**E.** Answer the question based on the map.

请问，从公园到电脑中心怎么走？

_____

_____

_____

**F.** Translate the following into Chinese. (PRESENTATIONAL)

**1. A:** Have you found your red shoes?

_____

**B:** No, I haven't.

_____

**A:** I heard your red shoes were expensive. A hundred dollars?

_____

**B:** Not that expensive.

_____

**2. A:** Have you finished the letter to your mother?

_____

**B:** No, I haven't finished. I haven't even started yet.

_____

**A:** Hurry up, her birthday is coming.

_____

**B:** Okay, I'll do it after I finish drinking this cup of coffee.

_____

3. **A:** Have you been to Chinatown?

   _____

   **B:** No, never. Where is it?

   _____

   **A:** It's not far from here. After two traffic lights, make a right turn, and you will be there. Would you like to go?

   _____

   **B:** Yes.

   _____

   **A:** Okay, let's go now.

   _____

4. **A:** I am going to order the hot and sour soup today. What would you like to order?

   _____

   **B:** I've had their hot and sour soup before. It is a bit sour and a bit spicy. Quite delicious. But I've never had dumplings here. I am going to order some dumplings.

   _____

   _____

   _____

## G. Storytelling (PRESENTATIONAL)

Write a story based on the four cartoons below. Make sure that your story has a beginning, middle, and end. Also, make sure that the transition from one picture to the next is smooth and logical.

**1**

**2**

**3**

**4**

# 14

## LESSON 14   Birthday Party
第十四课 生日晚会

---

**PART ONE**   Dialogue I: Let's Go to a Party!

## I. Listening Comprehension

### A. Textbook Dialogue (Multiple Choice) (INTERPRETIVE)

( )**1.** Whose birthday is it?

   **a.** Gao Wenzhong's cousin's
   **b.** Gao Wenzhong's
   **c.** Gao Xiaoyin's
   **d.** Gao Xiaoyin's boyfriend's

( )**2.** What will the host of the party *not* receive from Wang Peng and Li You?

   **a.** flowers
   **b.** fruit
   **c.** beverages
   **d.** balloons

( )**3.** What will the host and guests *not* do at the party?

   **a.** sing
   **b.** dance
   **c.** watch a DVD
   **d.** eat

( )**4.** Who will *not* be at the party?

   **a.** Gao Xiaoyin's boyfriend
   **b.** Gao Xiaoyin's classmate
   **c.** Gao Xiaoyin's cousin
   **d.** Gao Xiaoyin's parents

### B. Workbook Narrative (INTERPRETIVE)

Answer the following question after listening to the short passage:

Who bought what? Match each of the persons with the right kind(s) of fruit:

### C. Listening Rejoinder (INTERPERSONAL)

In this section, you will hear two speakers talking. After hearing the first speaker, select the best from the four possible responses given by the second speaker.

## II. Speaking Exercises

**A.** Answer the questions in Chinese based on the Textbook Dialogue. (INTERPRETIVE/PRESENTATIONAL)

1.  Why did Li You call Wang Peng?
2.  What will people do at Gao Xiaoyin's place?
3.  What will Wang Peng bring?
4.  What will Li You bring and why?
5.  How will Li You get to Gao Xiaoyin's place and why?

**B.** Do a role play with a partner. Invite your partner to your birthday party. Tell him/her when and where the party is, what people will do, what to bring, and how to get there. Ask your friend if he/she needs a ride. (INTERPERSONAL)

**C.** Tell your classmates about your favorite birthday party (including when and where the party was, what people did, and the reasons why it was your favorite). (PRESENTATIONAL)

# III. Reading Comprehension (INTERPRETIVE)

## A. Building Words

If you combine the *rè* in *tiānqi rè* with the *yǐn* in *yǐnliào*, you have *rèyǐn*, as seen in #1 below. Can you guess what the word *rèyǐn* means? Complete this section by providing the characters, the *pinyin*, and the English equivalent of each new word formed this way. You may consult a dictionary if necessary.

|  | | new word | *pinyin* | English |
|---|---|---|---|---|
| 1. | "天气热"的"热" + "饮料"的"饮" | | | |
| | → 热+饮 → _____ | _____ | _____ | |
| 2. | "天气冷"的"冷" + "饮料"的"饮" | | | |
| | → 冷+饮 → _____ | _____ | _____ | |
| 3. | "英国"的"国" + "一把花"的"花" | | | |
| | → 国+花 → _____ | _____ | _____ | |
| 4. | "门" + "路口"的"口" | | | |
| | → 门+口 → _____ | _____ | _____ | |
| 5. | "一把花"的"花" + "汽车"的"车" | | | |
| | → 花+车 → _____ | _____ | _____ | |

**B.** Read the following passage and answer the questions.

　　昨天是小常二十岁生日，晚上我们在他的宿舍给他过生日。小常的女朋友带了水果、饮料，还有很多好吃的东西。大家一边吃东西、一边聊天儿、一边玩，晚上十二点才回家，因为我昨天回家太晚，所以今天的考试考得糟糕极了。

Questions (True/False)

( ) **1.** Little Chang celebrated his nineteenth birthday last year.
( ) **2.** Little Chang's girlfriend prepared snacks, fruit, and drinks for the party.
( ) **3.** Everyone danced and had a great time last night.
( ) **4.** The narrator didn't go to bed until after midnight.
( ) **5.** The narrator did well on today's test.

**C.** Read the following dialogue and answer the questions.

（在李友的生日舞会上）

李友：小兰，喝点儿饮料或者吃点儿水果吧。

小兰：谢谢，我喝茶吧。李友，你看，张英正在跳舞呢。她穿的就是上个周末跟你一起买的那件衬衫，真漂亮。

李友：不对，她跟我一起买的那件是黄的。这件是白的，是你送给她的。你怎么忘了？

小兰：是啊，我怎么忘了呢？现在我知道我为什么这么喜欢这件衬衫了。

Questions (True/False)

( ) **1.** Little Lan likes tea better than soda pop.
( ) **2.** Li You went shopping with Zhang Ying last weekend.
( ) **3.** Zhang Ying is wearing a yellow blouse for the party.
( ) **4.** Zhang Ying bought a white blouse last weekend.
( ) **5.** Little Lan forgot to give Zhang Ying a present.

**D.** This is the menu of a multi-course meal. Take a look and answer the following questions.

# A套

凉菜： 鲜椒口水鸡

热拌时蔬

五香牛肉

糯米藕夹

蒜泥白肉

乡巴佬豆干

热菜： 鲜椒美极虾

香酥樟茶鸭

宫保带子

水煮鲶鱼

剁椒粉丝扇贝

烧汁牛柳

豆瓣肘子

榄菜季豆鸡掌脆

草菇扒菜胆

竹笋炖老鸡

小吃： 鸡汁锅贴

醪糟汤圆

水果拼盘

自制饮料两扎

**1.** Does the meal come with fruit and beverages? How do you know? _____

**2.** What do 凉菜 and 热菜 refer to? _____

# IV. Writing Exercises

**A.** Answer the following questions based on your own preferences.

1. 你爱吃什么水果？

   _____

2. 你爱喝什么饮料？

   _____

3. 你爱吃什么中国菜？

   _____

**B.** Ask and answer questions based on the illustrations given.

EXAMPLE:

→A: 她（正在）做什么呢？    B: 她（正在）跳舞呢。

1.

2. _____

   _____

3. _____

   _____

**C.** You are planning a party and telling people what to bring.

EXAMPLE:  → 王朋，请你带蛋糕 (dàngāo)。

1. _____

2. _____

3. _____

**D.** Little Fei is an effusive guy. For example, he likes to say about the place he lives

→ <u>我住的地方好极了</u> 。 (It's never just good, or even very good.)

What would he be likely to say about the following? Be sure to use a different adjective for each sentence:

**1.** the car he drives

**2.** the computer he uses

**3.** the characters he writes

**4.** the friends he knows

**E.** Translate the following into Chinese. (PRESENTATIONAL)

**1. A:** What kind of fruit do you like? Watermelon, pear, or apple?

**B:** I love to eat watermelon in the summer, and apples in the fall.

**2. A:** What are you doing?

**B:** I'm watching TV.

**A:** Gao Wenzhong is having a dance party. Do you feel like going?

**B:** Sure, but his place is very far from my house. Can you come pick me up?

**A:** No problem.

**B:** Thanks. I'll wait for you downstairs in ten minutes.

## PART TWO — Dialogue II: Attending a Birthday Party

# I. Listening Comprehension

### A. Textbook Dialogue (Multiple Choice) (INTERPRETIVE)

( ) **1.** Who greeted Wang Peng and Li You at the door?

  **a.** Gao Wenzhong
  **b.** Gao Wenzhong's cousin
  **c.** Gao Xiaoyin
  **d.** Bai Ying'ai

( ) **2.** Who hadn't arrived yet?

  **a.** Wang Hong
  **b.** Helen
  **c.** Tom
  **d.** Bai Ying'ai

( ) **3.** Who is Tom?

  **a.** Helen's dog
  **b.** Helen's son
  **c.** Helen's boyfriend
  **d.** Helen's cousin

( ) **4.** Helen speaks Chinese very well because

  **a.** she is Chinese.
  **b.** she was a Chinese teacher.
  **c.** she studied Chinese in summer school.
  **d.** she has a lot of Chinese friends.

### B. Workbook Dialogue (Multiple Choice) (INTERPRETIVE)

( ) **1.** The female speaker is the male speaker's _____.

  **a.** mother
  **b.** sister
  **c.** girlfriend
  **d.** cousin

( ) **2.** A book wouldn't be a good idea because

   **a.** the speaker's father doesn't have time to read.

   **b.** the speaker's father doesn't like to read.

   **c.** the speaker's father can't read.

   **d.** the speaker's father has too many books already.

( ) **3.** Coffee wouldn't make a good gift because

   **a.** the speaker's father doesn't like coffee.

   **b.** the speaker's father decided to give up caffeine.

   **c.** the speaker's father stopped drinking coffee on doctor's orders.

   **d.** the speaker's father is very picky about the coffee he drinks.

( ) **4.** A shirt wouldn't make a good present either because

   **a.** the speaker's father doesn't like others to buy clothes for him.

   **b.** the speaker's father doesn't wear dress shirts.

   **c.** the speaker's father doesn't need another shirt.

   **d.** it is impossible to find the right size for the father.

( ) **5.** What would the father like to have for his birthday?

   **a.** movies

   **b.** Chinese food

   **c.** time with his children

   **d.** time by himself

## C. Workbook Narrative (INTERPRETIVE)

The speaker left a phone message for her dog sitter. You are going to hear part of the message. After listening to it, answer the following questions in English.

1. Does the speaker already know the dog sitter? How do you know?

   _____

2. What specific instructions does the speaker give to the dog sitter? Please list them in detail.

   _____

3. If you were the dog sitter, would you have any questions for the owner? Ask at least one.

   _____

4. Has the dog sitter ever met the dog? How do you know?

   _____

**5.** Would you dog-sit for the speaker if you were asked? Why or why not?

## D. Listening Rejoinder (INTERPERSONAL)

In this section, you will hear two speakers talking. After hearing the first speaker, select the best from the four possible responses given by the second speaker.

# II. Speaking Exercises

**A.** Answer the questions in Chinese based on the Textbook Dialogue. (INTERPRETIVE/PRESENTATIONAL)

1. What did Gao Xiaoyin say when she received the birthday presents from Li You and Wang Peng?

2. How much time does Wang Hong spend practicing English every day?

3. Who is Tom?

4. Where did Helen study Chinese?

5. What does Tom look like?

**B.** Work with a partner and ask each other how long you normally eat dinner, do homework, and sleep every day. (INTERPERSONAL)

**C.** Work with a partner and ask each other which year you were born in, where you were born, and your Chinese zodiac sign. (INTERPERSONAL)

**D.** Show a photo of someone famous, a family member, or a friend, and describe to your classmates what the person looks like. (PRESENTATIONAL)

## III. Reading Comprehension (INTERPRETIVE)

### A. Building Words

If you combine the *yǎn* in *yǎnjing* with the *qiú* in *dǎ qiú*, you have *yǎnqiú*, as seen in #1 below. Can you guess what the word *yǎnqiú* means? Complete this section by providing the characters, the *pinyin*, and the English equivalent of each new word formed this way. You may consult a dictionary if necessary.

|  | new word | *pinyin* | English |
|---|---|---|---|
| 1. "眼睛"的"眼" + "打球"的"球" → 眼+球 → | _____ | _____ | _____ |
| 2. "鼻子"的"鼻" + "发音"的"音" → 鼻+音 → | _____ | _____ | _____ |
| 3. "蛋糕"的"蛋" + "白色"的"白" → 蛋+白 → | _____ | _____ | _____ |
| 4. "蛋糕"的"蛋" + "黄色"的"黄" → 蛋+黄 → | _____ | _____ | _____ |
| 5. "天气热"的"热" + "狗" → 热+狗 → | _____ | _____ | _____ |

**B.** Read the following passage and answer the questions.

张英很喜欢日文班的一个男同学。他们是在一个朋友的生日舞会上认识的，他们在一起聊天聊了半个多钟头。那个男同学跟张英一样，是英国人。他的眼睛大大的，鼻子高高的，笑的时候很好看。他又会唱歌又会跳舞。下个星期六学校有个舞会，张英很想请他一起去跳舞，可是不好意思问他。下午下课以后张英回宿舍，和她住在一起的李友说："刚才日文班的一个男的给你打电话，请你下个星期六和他一起去跳舞，可是我忘了他姓什么了。"张英听了以后，有点儿高兴，也有点儿紧张，她希望打电话的就是自己喜欢的那位男同学。

Questions (True/False)

(  )1. 张英喜欢的男孩子是她的朋友的朋友。

(  )2. 那个男孩子学习日文。

(  )3. 张英是英国人，可是那个男孩子是日本人。

(  )4. 张英想请那个男孩子来她家跳舞。

(  )5. 张英和李友今天上的课是一样的。

(  )6. 李友知道打电话的那个人是日文班的学生。

(  )7. 张英知道请她跳舞的那个人就是她喜欢的那个
男孩子。

**C.** Read the following dialogue and answer the questions.

（在李友的生日舞会上）

李友：哎，王朋，你怎么现在才来？

王朋：对不起，我来晚了。李友，这是我送给你的生日
礼物。

李友：谢谢。

王朋：还有一个礼物。

李友：哎，这是我忘在图书馆的中文书！太好了！你是什
么时候找到的？

王朋：刚找到的。

李友：你是怎么找到的？

王朋：我有一个朋友，在图书馆工作。他帮我找，我们一起找了两个多小时才找到。

李友：在哪儿找到的？

王朋：在日文书那边。图书馆里的人不认识中文，他们觉得中文跟日文一样。虽然你在书上写了你的中文名字，可是他们不认识那两个字。

李友：王朋，你真好。

Questions (True/False)

( ) **1.** Li You was anxiously awaiting Wang Peng's arrival.

( ) **2.** Wang Peng may have spent at least two hours in the library today.

( ) **3.** Wang Peng spent a lot of money on his second birthday gift for Li You.

( ) **4.** Wang Peng had told Li You that he would look for her lost book.

Questions (Multiple Choice)

( ) **5.** Wang Peng went to look for the book today because _____.

   **a.** he wanted to make Li You happy on her birthday

   **b.** he knew his librarian friend was working today

   **c.** he wanted to save money on a birthday gift

( ) **6.** The librarians hadn't found the book earlier because _____.

   **a.** Li You didn't write her name on it as she said

   **b.** they couldn't tell written Chinese from written Japanese

   **c.** they knew that Wang Peng would find it anyway

**D.** Read the passage, answer the questions in English, and draw a picture based on the passage.

这是我的狗，他的毛 (máo, hair; fur) 是黑色的，我叫他小黑。因为我属狗，所以我爸爸妈妈送小黑给我做生日礼物。他长得很可爱，脸大大的，嘴小小的，鼻子不高。

我常常带他到公园去玩。他跟我一样，也喜欢吃肉，喝饮料，不喜欢运动，每天晚上也睡九个钟头的觉。你看，这是小黑的照片，他正在笑呢！

1. What's the dog's name? Who gave him that name, and why?
2. Why did the narrator's parents give her a dog as her birthday gift?
3. What do you know about the narrator from the passage?

**E.** What does this store sell? What kind of discount does it offer? _____

# IV. Writing Exercises

## A. Building Characters

Form a character by fitting the given components together as indicated. Then provide a word or phrase in which that character appears.

EXAMPLE: 左边一个"女"，右边一个"子"

是_"好久不见"_的_"好"_。

1. 左边一个"女"，右边一个"而且"的"且"是

    _____的_____。

2. 左边一个"纟"，右边一个"工作"的"工"是

    _____的_____。

3. 上边一个"日"，下边一个"或者"的"者"是

    _____的_____。

4. 左边一个"工作"的"工"，右边一个"力"是

    _____的_____。

5. 左边一个"目"，右边一个"青菜"的"青"是

    _____的_____。

**B.** Your friend is studying apparel merchandising and would like to interview you for a marketing class assignment. Answer the following questions based on what you are wearing today.

1. 你的衣服是什么时候买的？

    _____

2. 你的衣服是在哪儿买的？

    _____

3. 你的衣服是谁买的？

_____

4. 你的衣服是花多少钱买的？

_____

**C.** Answer the following questions based on your own situation.

1. **A:** 你平常每天做功课做多长时间？

   **B:** _____ 。

   **A:** 昨天呢？

   **B:** _____ 。

2. **A:** 你平常吃晚饭吃多长时间？

   **B:** _____ 。

   **A:** 昨天呢？

   **B:** _____ 。

3. **A:** 你平常洗澡洗多长时间？

   **B:** _____ 。

   **A:** 昨天呢？

   **B:** _____ 。

**D.** Describe the dog in the picture. Include as many details as you can. (PRESENTATIONAL)

**E.** Describe what you hope your ideal boyfriend/girlfriend would look like. (PRESENTATIONAL)

**F.** Translate the following into Chinese. (PRESENTATIONAL)

**1.** **A:** Little Li is a good student. He is smart and hardworking.

_____

**B:** I heard he does homework for four hours every night.

_____

**A:** But he likes to exercise, too. We exercised for an hour yesterday afternoon at the student center.

_____

_____

**B:** Really? He is quite busy.

_____

**2.** **A:** Who's that guy skating?

_____

**B:** That's my boyfriend, Tom.

_____

**A:** He's quite handsome. Is he older or younger than you?

_____

**B:** He's the same age as I am. We were both born in 1990.

_____

**A:** Where did you meet?

_____

**B:** We met in the park.

_____

3. The man who is cooking over there is my older brother. My mother used to say that my older brother was smart and hardworking, and that he would be a great lawyer like her after he grew up. But my older brother is not a lawyer. He likes to cook, and the food he makes is extremely good. He now works in a restaurant. He is not like my mother at all.

**G.** You are planning a birthday party for your best friend. Please write up a plan for the guest of honor to review. The plan needs to include information such as whom you are inviting, where the party takes place, what people can bring to the party, what activities there will be, how long each activity will last, and what gifts your friend might wish to receive. Some of the party guests may need a ride to the party; include suggestions for their travel plans. (PRESENTATIONAL)

## H. Storytelling (PRESENTATIONAL)

Write a story in Chinese based on the four cartoons below. Make sure that your story has a beginning, middle, and end. Also make sure that the transition from one picture to the next is smooth and logical.

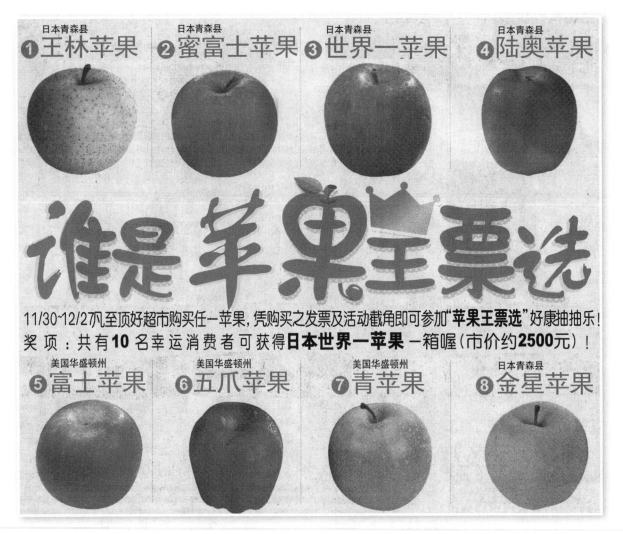

你喜欢吃哪种苹果？

# 15 LESSON 15  Seeing a Doctor
## 第十五课 看病

**PART ONE**  ## Dialogue I: My Stomachache Is Killing Me!

## I. Listening Comprehension

### A. Textbook Dialogue (Multiple Choice) (INTERPRETIVE)

( )  **1.** Gao Wenzhong has not been feeling well since_____.

    **a.** last week

    **b.** five days ago

    **c.** yesterday morning

    **d.** last night

( )  **2.** Gao Wenzhong has a stomachache because _____.

    **a.** he had too much ice

    **b.** he has an ulcer

    **c.** he ate some spoiled food

    **d.** he drank polluted water

( )  **3.** Gao Wenzhong needs to take _____.

    **a.** three pills twice a day

    **b.** two pills three times a day

    **c.** one pill three times a day

    **d.** two pills twice a day

( )  **4.** The doctor recommends that Gao Wenzhong _____.

    **a.** abstain from food for twenty-four hours

    **b.** drink nothing but water for twenty-four hours

    **c.** rest for twenty-four hours

    **d.** come back to the clinic in twenty-four hours

### B. Workbook Narrative (INTERPRETIVE)

Answer the following questions after listening to the short passage:

**1.** What is the dog's name? Why do you think it has a name like that?

_____

**2.** What does the speaker do annually to care for the dog? List two things.

_____

**3.** What is the good news about the dog?

_____

**4.** What is the bad news about the dog? List two things.

_____

**5.** What did the doctor tell the speaker *not* to do?

_____

### C. Listening Rejoinder (INTERPERSONAL)

In this section, you will hear two speakers talking. After hearing the first speaker, select the best from the four possible responses given by the second speaker.

_____

# II. Speaking Exercises

**A.** Answer the questions in Chinese based on the Textbook Dialogue. (INTERPRETIVE/PRESENTATIONAL)

**1.** Why did Gao Wenzhong go to the doctor?

**2.** How did his symptoms start?

**3.** What did the doctor say about the cause of his illness?

**4.** What were the instructions on his prescription?

**5.** What did the doctor suggest Gao Wenzhong should do in addition to taking the prescription?

**B.** With a partner, do a role play as a doctor and a patient. The patient describes his/her symptoms and asks the doctor about the treatment. The doctor responds and gives instructions based on the label below. (INTERPERSONAL)

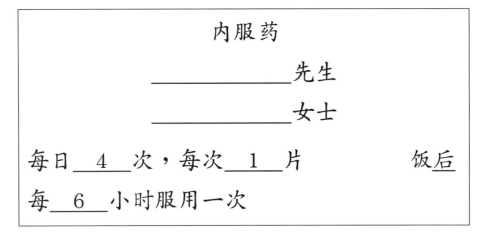

```
                        内服药

            _____先生

            _____女士

    每日 __4__ 次，每次 __1__ 片           饭后

    每 __6__ 小时服用一次
```

## III. Reading Comprehension (INTERPRETIVE)

### A. Building Words

If you combine the *zhōng* in *Zhōngguó* with the *yī* in *yīshēng*, you have *zhōngyī*, as seen in #1 below. Can you guess what the word *zhōngyī* means? Complete this section by providing the characters, the pinyin, and the English equivalent of each new word formed this way. You may consult a dictionary if necessary.

|  |  | new word | *pinyin* | English |
|---|---|---|---|---|

1. "中国" 的 "中" + "医生" 的 "医"

   → 中+医 → _____  _____  _____

2. "东南西北" 的 "西" + "医生" 的 "医"

   → 西+医 → _____  _____  _____

3. "公共汽车" 的 "公" + "厕所" 的 "厕"

   → 公+厕 → _____  _____  _____

4. "写信" 的 "信" + "冰箱" 的 "箱"

   → 信+箱 → _____  _____  _____

5. "吃药" 的 "药" + "检查" 的 "检"

   → 药+检 → _____  _____  _____

**B.** Read the following passage and answer the questions.

因为今天要考试，小黄昨天晚上把功课做完以后就开始看书，今天早上四点才睡觉，六点就起床了。一起床他就觉得头有一点儿疼。考完试以后，小黄头越来越疼，就去看医生。医生说小黄没什么问题，只是睡觉不够，今天晚上多睡一点就好了。医生没有给他打针，也没给他药吃。

Questions (True/False)

( ) 1. 小黄昨天晚上先做功课，然后看书。

( ) 2. 因为小黄考试考得不好，所以他头疼。

( ) 3. 考试以后，小黄的头比起床的时候更疼了。

( ) 4. 医生觉得小黄的病很重。

( ) 5. 医生告诉小黄今天晚上得多睡觉。

( ) 6. 医生觉得小黄不用打针，也不用吃药。

**C.** Read the following passage and answer the questions.

小钱以前住在学生宿舍，每天在学生餐厅吃饭。餐厅的菜很便宜，可是不好吃，小钱常常吃很少一点东西就不想吃了。小钱妈妈知道了，就说，"回家来住吧。"这个学期小钱住在家里，每天都吃妈妈做的菜，觉得好吃极了。小钱家离学校很远，她每天早上很早就得起床，然后坐地铁去上课。因为她睡觉睡得不够，眼睛常常是红红的，有点儿不舒服。可是小钱还是觉得住在家里比住在学生宿舍好。

Questions (True/False):

( )**1.**  Little Qian has been living at home for a year.

( )**2.**  When she lived on campus, Little Qian had to spend a lot of money on food.

( )**3.**  Little Qian's mother is a good cook.

( )**4.**  Little Qian's eyes are often uncomfortable because of some kind of allergy.

( )**5.**  We can assume that Little Qian will not move back to the dorm soon.

**D.** Read the following passage and answer the questions.

　　李友星期四晚上请王红教她做了一盘家常豆腐，没吃完，就把没吃完的豆腐放在冰箱里了。星期五李友吃早饭，吃了几口豆腐，上课的时候肚子就疼起来了。李友一下课就去看医生，医生检查了一下，说是吃坏肚子了。李友不懂那盘豆腐在冰箱里只放了八、九个小时，怎么会把肚子吃坏了呢？她打电话请王朋来帮她看看冰箱，王朋检查了以后说："冰箱坏了。"

Questions (True/False)

( )**1.**  Li You cooked a tofu dish and invited Wang Hong to dinner.

( )**2.**  The tofu dish was the cause of Li You's stomachache.

( )**3.**  When Li You went to the doctor, it took the doctor a long time to diagnose the problem.

( )**4.**  Until she saw the doctor, Li You had taken for granted that her refrigerator was functioning properly.

( )**5.**  Li You asked Wang Peng to help her look for a new refrigerator.

**E.** This is an instruction label on a prescription drug bottle. Explain in Chinese what you think the character "服" means.

_____

| 姓名 |
|---|
| 日期 |

每日服 ........... 次，每次服 .......... 粒
每隔 .......... 小时服1次

☐ 空 肚 服        ☐ 饱 肚 服

☐ 早 上 服        ☐ 睡 前 服

☐ 咬 碎 服        ☐ 含 口 服

☐ 发 烧 服        ☐ 需要时服

☐ 服药后可能会有睡意、忌驾驶、忌饮酒

| 药名 |
|---|

# IV. Writing Exercises

**A.** Ask and answer questions based on the illustrations given.

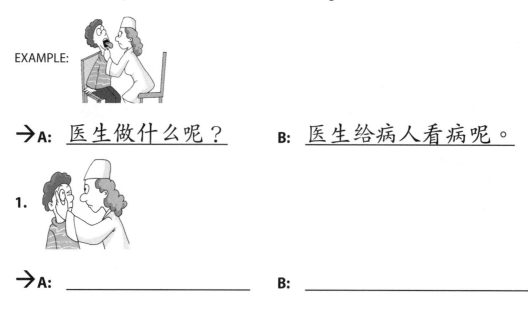

EXAMPLE:

→A: 医生做什么呢？    B: 医生给病人看病呢。

1.

→A: _____    B: _____

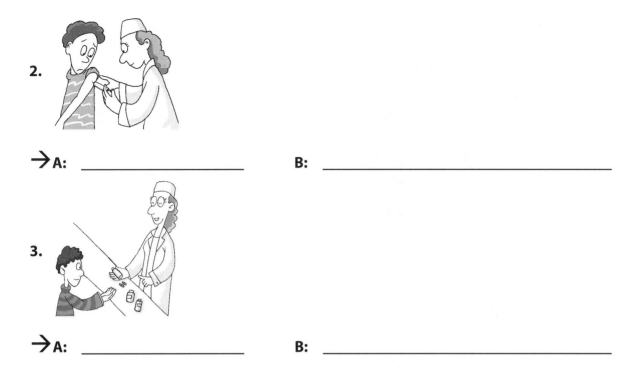

**2.**

→A: _____   B: _____

**3.**

→A: _____   B: _____

**B.** Answer the following questions based on your own situation.

1. 你每个星期上几次中文课？

_____

2. 你每个星期工作几次？

_____

3. 你每个星期运动几次？

_____

4. 你每个月洗几次衣服？

_____

5. 你昨天喝了几次水？

_____

**C.** Imagine that your younger brother is coming to stay with you for a few weeks. You need to let him know how to keep the house in order and tell him where he can place his things.

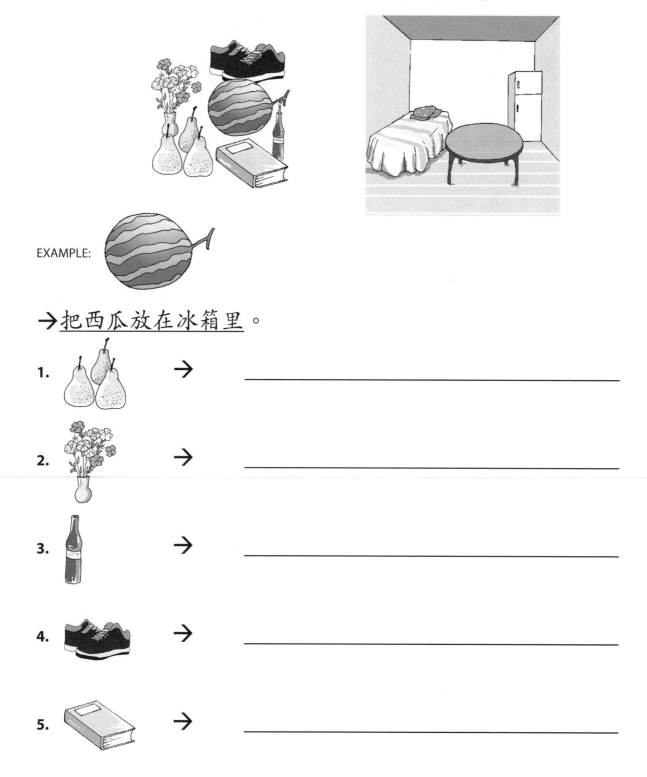

EXAMPLE:

→ 把西瓜放在冰箱里。

1. →  _____

2. →  _____

3. →  _____

4. →  _____

5. →  _____

**D.** What does your teacher often say to the class?

EXAMPLE: Please hand in your homework.    →    <u>请把功课给我</u>。

1.   Please finish your homework.    →    _____

2.   Please finish listening to the audio.    →    _____

3.   Please write the characters correctly.    →    _____

**E.** Translate the following into Chinese. (PRESENTATIONAL)

1.   **A:**   Where is the watermelon I bought?

_____

**B:**   I put it in the refrigerator.

_____

2.   **A:**   I drank three glasses of water before bed last night, and I went to the bathroom twice late last night.

_____

**B:**   You'd better not drink any water before bed.

_____

3.   The teacher asked us to listen to the audio recording ten times every day. But I often listen to it three times. Last night, I only listened once. I hope the teacher won't ask me to read the text aloud today. I will definitely do a very bad job.

_____

_____

_____

_____

This is the name of an over-the-counter medicine. What is it for?

## PART TWO    Dialogue II: Allergies

### I. Listening Comprehension

**A. Textbook Dialogue** (Multiple Choice) (INTERPRETIVE)

(   ) **1.** Wang Peng's eyes are red because _____.

    **a.** they are infected

    **b.** he is suffering from allergies

    **c.** he has been crying

    **d.** he is wearing contact lenses

(   ) **2.** Wang Peng has been self-medicating because _____.

    **a.** he doesn't have health insurance

    **b.** he is too busy to see a doctor

    **c.** he has the right medicine

    **d.** he knows a lot about medicine

(   ) **3.** Li You thinks that Wang Peng should _____.

    **a.** take his illness more seriously

    **b.** be more careful with his money

    **c.** not be too reliant on pills

    **d.** not worry about his health incessantly

(   ) **4.** Li You offers to _____.

    **a.** buy some new medicine for Wang Peng

    **b.** lend Wang Peng some money for better health insurance

    **c.** go to the doctor's office with Wang Peng

    **d.** call a doctor friend for advice

**B. Workbook Narrative** (True/False) (INTERPRETIVE)

Answer the following questions after listening to the short telephone message:

(   ) **1.** The message was left by the caller on her brother's answering machine.

(   ) **2.** The caller's mother called today.

(   ) **3.** The mother doesn't know that her son is suffering from allergies.

(   ) **4.** The caller assumes her brother will seek treatment this morning.

(   ) **5.** The caller wants her brother to call their mother.

(   ) **6.** The caller would like to see a Chinese film tomorrow.

### C. Listening Rejoinder (INTERPERSONAL)

In this section, you will hear two speakers talking. After hearing the first speaker, select the best from the four possible responses given by the second speaker.

_____

# II. Speaking Exercises

**A.** Answer the questions in Chinese based on the Textbook Dialogue. (INTERPRETIVE/PRESENTATIONAL)

1. What are Wang Peng's symptoms?
2. What does Li You think Wang Peng's problem is?
3. Where did Wang Peng get his medication?
4. Why doesn't Wang Peng see a doctor?
5. What does Wang Peng plan to do about his illness?

**B.** With a partner, discuss what each of you does when you have a cold (such as seeing a doctor, taking medicine, resting and staying home from school or work, or other ways of recuperating). (INTERPERSONAL)

**C.** With a partner, do a role play. You are feeling ill, but you don't feel like seeing a doctor. Describe your symptoms and explain why you don't want to go to the doctor. Your partner tries his/her best to persuade you to see a doctor. (INTERPERSONAL)

# III. Reading Comprehension (INTERPRETIVE)

## A. Building Words

If you combine the *bìng* in *shēng bìng* with the *chuáng* in *qǐ chuáng*, you have *bìngchuáng*, as seen in #1 below. Can you guess what the word *bìngchuáng* means together as a word? Complete this section by providing the characters, the *pinyin*, and the English equivalent of each new word formed this way. You may consult a dictionary if necessary.

|  | | new word | pinyin | English |
|---|---|---|---|---|
| 1. | "生病" 的 "病" + "起床" 的 "床" <br> → 病+床 → | | _____ | _____ | _____ |
| 2. | "生病" 的 "病" + "寒假" 的 "假" <br> → 病+假 → | | _____ | _____ | _____ |

3. "身体"的"身"＋"高"

   → 身＋高 → ＿＿＿＿＿＿ ＿＿＿＿＿＿ ＿＿＿＿＿＿

4. "身体"的"体"＋"检查"的"检"

   → 体＋检 → ＿＿＿＿＿＿ ＿＿＿＿＿＿ ＿＿＿＿＿＿

5. "身体"的"体"＋"重"

   → 体＋重 → ＿＿＿＿＿＿ ＿＿＿＿＿＿ ＿＿＿＿＿＿

**B.** Read the following passage and answer the questions.

医生：你哪儿不舒服？

病人：医生，我肚子疼死了。

医生：我给你检查一下。你昨天吃什么东西了？

病人：我昨天晚上吃了一盘糖醋鱼和几个饺子。

医生：我知道了，一定是那盘糖醋鱼有问题。你得赶快吃药，要不然你的肚子会越来越疼。你去的那个饭馆一定很便宜，对不对？你以后出去吃饭，一定要去贵的饭馆。虽然多付一点钱，可是你吃了不会生病。

病人：您说得对，那家饭馆很便宜，可是我觉得那盘鱼真的很好吃，不会有问题。

医生：你是在哪个饭馆吃的？

病人：在我们学校南边的那家小饭馆。

医生：是吗？…哎，糟糕了！

病人：医生，您怎么了？

医生：我的肚子也疼起来了，昨天晚上我也是在那家饭馆
　　　吃的晚饭。

Questions (True/False)

( )   **1.**   The patient and the doctor meet in a restaurant.

( )   **2.**   The patient has a stomachache.

( )   **3.**   Neither the doctor nor the patient had dinner at home yesterday.

( )   **4.**   The doctor urges the patient to take medicine as soon as possible.

( )   **5.**   The doctor always dines at expensive restaurants.

Questions (Multiple Choice)

( )   **6.**   What is the doctor's logic as he tries to diagnose the patient's problem?

    **a.**   If the food was the problem, the restaurant must have been cheap.

    **b.**   If the patient got a stomachache, he must have eaten spoiled fish.

    **c.**   If a restaurant is cheap, it must have served cheap fish dishes.

( )   **7.**   What is the doctor's advice to the patient about dining out?

    **a.**   Go to more expensive restaurants where the food is tastier.

    **b.**   Go to more reputable restaurants where the food is more expensive.

    **c.**   Go to more expensive restaurants where the food is safer.

( )   **8.**   What can we say about the doctor?

    **a.**   He himself follows the advice he gives to his patient.

    **b.**   He himself does not follow the advice he gives to his patient.

    **c.**   He advises his patient to do things his way.

**C.** Read the following passage and answer the questions.

小高这几天一直不舒服。上个周末他头疼，医生给了
他一些药，他吃了两次就好了。可是星期一小高觉得鼻子
很痒，眼睛红红的。医生说他一定是对什么过敏了。医生
给了他一种药，可是小高吃了三天，一点儿用也没有。今
天上午小高又去看医生，想请医生给点儿别的药试试。医

生请他把他吃的药拿出来看看，才知道小高这几天吃的不是过敏药，是头疼药！

Questions (True/False)

( ) **1.** 小高上个周末和这个星期都不太舒服。

( ) **2.** 小高吃了头疼药，头很快就不疼了。

( ) **3.** 上个星期天小高把头疼药都吃完了。

( ) **4.** 医生说，小高对头疼药过敏，所以眼睛红红的。

( ) **5.** 星期三小高的眼睛不红了，鼻子也不痒了。

( ) **6.** 小高今天上午又去看医生，因为他觉得医生给他的过敏药没有用。

( ) **7.** 因为小高吃错药了，所以他的病还没好。

**D.** Read the following passage and answer the questions.

　　李友的朋友小钱很喜欢学校医院的一位男医生。小钱身体很健康，可是为了去看那位医生，就说自己鼻子痒，眼睛疼，一定是对什么过敏了。李友一边笑一边说："你平常不过敏，怎么一看到那位长得很帅的男医生眼睛就疼起来，鼻子就痒起来了?你一定是对那位医生过敏了。"

Questions (True/False)

( ) **1.** Little Qian first met the doctor when she went to the hospital for her allergy.
( ) **2.** According to Li You, Little Qian has suffered from her allergy for a long time.
( ) **3.** According to Li You, her allergy is Little Qian's excuse for visiting that doctor.
( ) **4.** Li You knows Little Qian very well.
( ) **5.** Little Qian's allergy symptoms become worse when she sees the doctor.
( ) **6.** Li You suggests that Little Qian should see a different doctor.

**E.** This is a form that a new patient needs to fill out. Locate the area asking if the patient has any allergic reactions to any drugs.

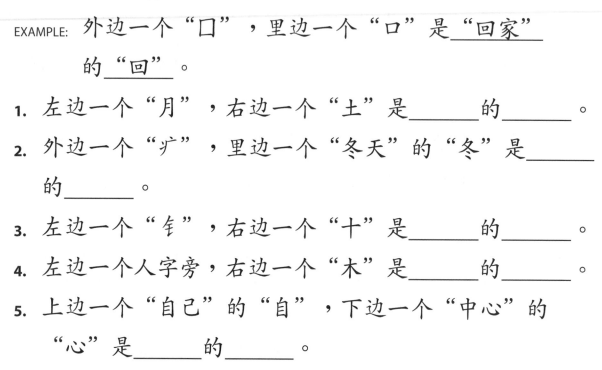

## IV. Writing Exercises

### A. Building Characters

Form a character by fitting the given components together as indicated. Then provide a word or phrase in which that character appears.

EXAMPLE:  外边一个"囗"，里边一个"口"是<u>"回家"</u>的<u>"回"</u>。

1.  左边一个"月"，右边一个"土"是_____的_____。

2.  外边一个"疒"，里边一个"冬天"的"冬"是_____的_____。

3.  左边一个"钅"，右边一个"十"是_____的_____。

4.  左边一个人字旁，右边一个"木"是_____的_____。

5.  上边一个"自己"的"自"，下边一个"中心"的"心"是_____的_____。

**B.** In Chinese, list possible symptoms of the following sicknesses.

1. 感冒： _____

2. 过敏： _____

3. 拉(lā)肚子(diarrhea)： _____

**C.** Explain in Chinese what each person is allergic to, based on the illustrations given.

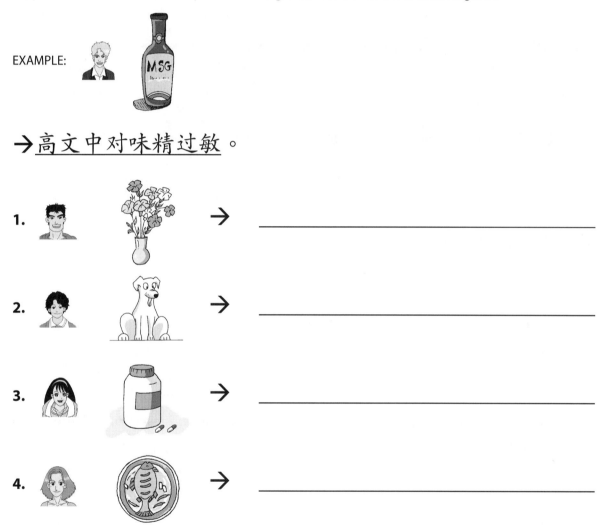

EXAMPLE:

→高文中对味精过敏。

1. →_____

2. →_____

3. →_____

4. →_____

**D.** Answer the following questions based on your own situation.

1. 最近天气越来越冷还是越来越暖和？

_____

2. 你的功课越来越多还是越来越少？

_____

3. 健康保险越来越贵还是越来越便宜？

_____

4. 找工作越来越容易还是越来越难？

_____

**E.** Translate the following into Chinese. (PRESENTATIONAL)

1. **A:** Do you have a fever?

_____

   **B:** I do, but I bought some medicine.

_____

   **A:** You can't just take any kind of medicine when you have a fever. You'd better see the doctor.

_____

_____

2. **A:** Take out the clothes you bought so I can take a look.

_____

   **B:** Here they are.

_____

**A:** Why did you buy these clothes?

_____

**B:** Because they fit well, and besides, they were cheap, too.

_____

**3. A:** What's the matter with you? Do you have a cold?

_____

**B:** My eyes are itchy. I think I am allergic to your dog.

_____

**A:** But you've been to my house five or six times...

_____

**B:** My eyes are getting itchier and itchier. Please hurry and give me a ride to see the doctor.

_____

**A:** I'll give you a ride if you have health insurance. Otherwise, how about having a little lie-down after you take this medicine that my doctor gave me?

_____

_____

## F. Storytelling (PRESENTATIONAL)

Write a story in Chinese based on the four cartoons below. Make sure that your story has a beginning, middle and end. Also make sure that the transition from one picture to the next is smooth and logical.

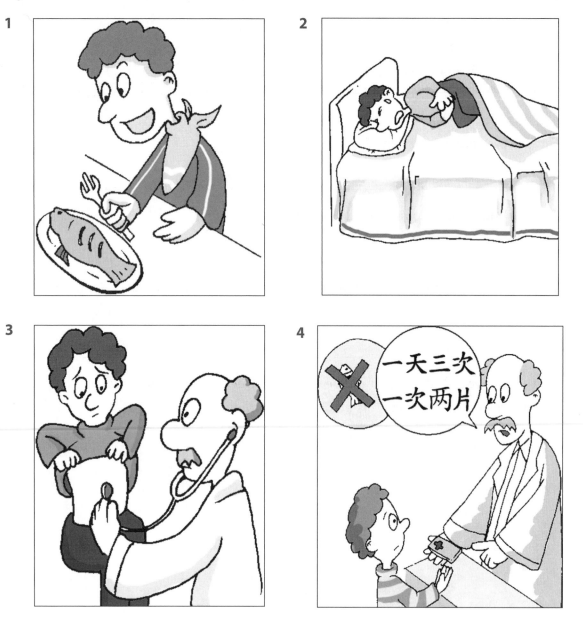

# Let's Review (LESSONS 11–15)

## I. How do we say these words/phrases?

Write down their correct pronunciation and tones in *pinyin*, and use a tape recorder or computer to record them. Hand in the recording to your teacher if asked.

1. 出去　　去年　　　　　　　＿＿＿＿＿　＿＿＿＿＿

2. 下雪　　下雨　　　　　　　＿＿＿＿＿　＿＿＿＿＿

3. 预报　　运动　　　　　　　＿＿＿＿＿　＿＿＿＿＿

4. 肚子　　舞会　　　　　　　＿＿＿＿＿　＿＿＿＿＿

5. 路口　　暑期班　　　　　　＿＿＿＿＿　＿＿＿＿＿

6. 糖醋鱼　红绿灯　　　　　　＿＿＿＿＿　＿＿＿＿＿

7. 牛肉　　水果　　　　　　　＿＿＿＿＿　＿＿＿＿＿

8. 远近　　越来越乱　我约你　＿＿＿＿＿　＿＿＿＿＿　＿＿＿＿＿

9. 不饿　　不渴　　　厕所　　＿＿＿＿＿　＿＿＿＿＿　＿＿＿＿＿

10. 楼下　　菜够了　　我属狗　＿＿＿＿＿　＿＿＿＿＿　＿＿＿＿＿

11. 长短　　长大　　　　　　　＿＿＿＿＿　＿＿＿＿＿

12. 觉得　　睡觉　　　　　　　＿＿＿＿＿　＿＿＿＿＿

## II. Group the characters according to their radicals, and provide the meaning of each radical.

肚　暖　冷　绿　桌　素　热

碟　醋　饿　暑　疼　冰　饺　约　槽　病　酸　糕

碗　精　灯　楼　脸　烧　痒　梨　饮

| Radical | Meaning of the Radical (English) | Characters |
|---|---|---|
| 1. _____ | _____ | _____ |
| 2. _____ | _____ | _____ |
| 3. _____ | _____ | _____ |
| 4. _____ | _____ | _____ |
| 5. _____ | _____ | _____ |
| 6. _____ | _____ | _____ |
| 7. _____ | _____ | _____ |
| 8. _____ | _____ | _____ |
| 9. _____ | _____ | _____ |
| 10. _____ | _____ | _____ |
| 11. _____ | _____ | _____ |

## III. VO or Not

Among the verbs below, distinguish those that are VO compounds from those that are not.

滑冰      下雪      点菜      检查

打针      看病      过敏      听说

**VO Compounds:** _____

**not VO Compounds:** _____

## IV. Have You Seen that Character Before?

Circle the character shared by the words in each group. Write down the *pinyin* for the character in common, and define the character's original meaning.

|  |  |  |  | *pinyin* | meaning |
|---|---|---|---|---|---|
| **1.** 预习 | 预报 | | | _____ | _____ |
| **2.** 常常 | 平常 | 非常 | 家常豆腐 | _____ | _____ |
| **3.** 售货员 | 服务员 | | | _____ | _____ |
| **4.** 考试 | 面试 | | | _____ | _____ |
| **5.** 糟糕 | 蛋糕 | | | _____ | _____ |
| **6.** 老师 | 师傅 | | | _____ | _____ |
| **7.** 黄色 | 黄瓜 | | | _____ | _____ |
| **8.** 黄瓜 | 西瓜 | | | _____ | _____ |
| **9.** 运动场 | 活动中心 | | | _____ | _____ |
| **10.** 飞机场 | 运动场 | | | _____ | _____ |
| **11.** 商店 | 书店 | | | _____ | _____ |
| **12.** 地图 | 图书馆 | | | _____ | _____ |
| **13.** 跳舞 | 舞会 | | | _____ | _____ |
| **14.** 水果 | 苹果 | | | _____ | _____ |

15. 功课　　　用功　　　　　　　　　_____　_____

16. 医生　　　医院　　　　　　　　　_____　_____

17. 冰茶　　　冰箱　　　　　　　　　_____　_____

18. 发烧　　　红烧牛肉　　　　　　　_____　_____

# V. Getting to Know You

Put your Chinese to use. Interview one of your classmates to find out more about him/her. After a brief Q & A session, jot down and organize the information you have gathered, and then present an oral or written report to introduce your classmate to the rest of the class. (INTERPERSONAL/ PRESENTATIONAL)

## A. Food Preferences and Habits

1. 你平常晚饭能吃几碗米饭？吃得下两碗吗？

2. 你先吃饭再喝汤还是先喝汤再吃饭？

3. 你吃素吗？

4. 你能不能吃辣的？

5. 要是你很饿，你想吃什么？

6. 你最爱喝什么饮料？

7. 你最爱吃什么水果？

8. 你做饭的时候放不放味精？

9. 你对味精过敏吗？

10. 要是你在饭馆点菜，但是你想吃的菜卖完了，你怎么办？

11. 你常常吃坏肚子吗？

12. 如果肚子疼，你怎么办？

...

**B. Clothing and Fashion**

你今天穿的衣服

　　是在哪儿买的？

　　是什么时候买的？

　　是谁买的？

　　是花多少钱买的？

你觉得衣服的大小、颜色、样子（对你）合适不合适？

…

**C. Living Situation and Commute**

1. 你的学校在你住的地方的哪一边？

2. 你的学校离你住的地方远不远？

3. 你去过学校的学生活动中心吗？在图书馆的哪一边？

4. 你平常几点去学校上课？今天呢？今天是几点去学校
上课的？

5. 你平常怎么去学校上课？今天呢？今天是怎么去学校
上课的？

**D. Academic Studies**

1. 你为什么上这个学校？

2. 你在这个学校学了多长时间了？

3. 你每个星期上几次中文课？每次上多长时间？

4. 你会用中文发电子邮件吗？

5. 你常常上网用中文跟人聊天儿吗？

**E. Dream Date**

1.  你希望你的男/女朋友长得怎么样？

2.  你希望你的男/女朋友是哪一年生的？属什么？

3.  你希望你的男/女朋友比你聪明、比你酷吗？

4.  如果你想约你的男/女朋友出去玩儿，你们会去什么
    地方？

# LESSON 16  **Dating**
第十六课 约会

**PART ONE**  **Dialogue I: Seeing a Movie**

## I. Listening Comprehension

### A. Textbook Dialogue (True/False) (INTERPRETIVE)

( ) **1.** Wang Peng and Li You have known each other for almost six months.

( ) **2.** There is a Chinese film at school tonight.

( ) **3.** Wang Peng will have a difficult time getting tickets to the film.

( ) **4.** Li You has seen many Chinese films before.

( ) **5.** Wang Peng and Li You will be going to the film with friends.

### B. Workbook Conversation (INTERPRETIVE)

Answer the following questions after listening to the conversation:

1. What does the man offer to do? List four things.

   a. _____

   b. _____

   c. _____

   d. _____

2. What are the four reasons that the woman gives for not accepting the man's invitations and offers?

   a. _____

   b. _____

**c.** _____

**d.** _____

3. What does the woman really want?

   _____

4. Does the man get the message?

   _____

## C. Listening Rejoinder (INTERPERSONAL)

In this section, you will hear two speakers talking. After hearing the first speaker, select the best from the four possible responses given by the second speaker.

_____

# II. Speaking Exercises

**A.** Answer the questions in Chinese based on the Textbook Dialogue. (INTERPRETIVE/PRESENTATIONAL)

1. How long have Li You and Wang Peng known each other?
2. How did Li You and Wang Peng become good friends?
3. What would Wang Peng like to invite Li You to do this weekend?
4. Was it easy for Wang Peng to get tickets? Why or why not?
5. What additional plans have Wang Peng and Li You made for the day of the event?

**B.** With a partner, do a role play. Invite your partner to go to the movies with you this weekend. Decide together which movie you should see, and discuss what you could do before and after the movie. (INTERPERSONAL)

**C.** My Best Friend: Tell your classmates how you met your best friend, how long you have known each other, why you like him/her, and what you usually do together. (PRESENTATIONAL)

# III. Reading Comprehension (INTERPRETIVE)

## A. Building Words

If you combine the *tóng* in *tóng yí ge* with the *bān* in *shǔqī bān*, you have *tóngbān*, as seen in #1 below. Can you guess what the word *tóngbān* means? Complete this section by providing the characters, the *pinyin*, and the English equivalent of each new word formed this way. You may consult a dictionary if necessary.

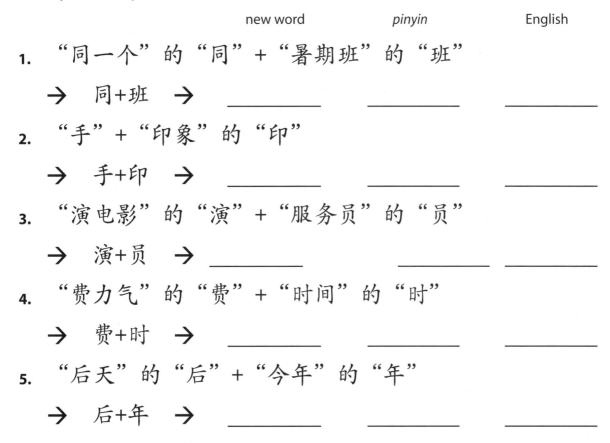

|  | new word | *pinyin* | English |
|---|---|---|---|
| 1. "同一个"的"同" + "暑期班"的"班" → 同+班 → | _____ | _____ | _____ |
| 2. "手" + "印象"的"印" → 手+印 → | _____ | _____ | _____ |
| 3. "演电影"的"演" + "服务员"的"员" → 演+员 → | _____ | _____ | _____ |
| 4. "费力气"的"费" + "时间"的"时" → 费+时 → | _____ | _____ | _____ |
| 5. "后天"的"后" + "今年"的"年" → 后+年 → | _____ | _____ | _____ |

**B.** Read the following passage and answer the questions.

　　小谢跟小黄认识已经快两年了，他们是英文班的同学。小黄去过英国，英文说得很好，常常帮小谢练习说英文。小黄做饭做得不太好，周末的时候，小谢常常请小黄到她家去吃饭。小黄对小谢的印象越来越好。小谢觉得小黄又聪明，又用功，对他的印象也很好。上个周末小谢的爸爸妈妈来看她，小谢把小黄介绍给爸妈认识。小谢的爸妈觉得小黄长得不错，学习也不错，很喜欢小黄。

Questions (True/False)

( ) **1.** 小谢的英文老师也是小黄的英文老师。

( ) **2.** 两年以前小谢不认识小黄。

( ) **3.** 小谢说英文说得比小黄好。

( ) **4.** 周末小谢常常请小黄到饭馆去吃饭。

( ) **5.** 小黄觉得小谢是个很好的女孩子。

( ) **6.** 小谢喜欢小黄，但小谢的爸妈觉得他们在一起不合适。

**C.** Read the following passage and answer the questions.

高文中对白英爱印象很好，可是他不知道白英爱对他印象怎么样，所以一直没有告诉姐姐高小音他喜欢白英爱，朋友们也都不知道。高小音问他喜欢什么样的女孩子，文中说："眼睛大大的，鼻子高高的，嘴不大也不小。得聪明，会跳舞，还会做饭。"小音觉得要找到这么好的女孩子，得费很大力气。高文中又说："那个女孩子最好姓白。"小音才知道高文中说的一定是白英爱。

Questions:

**1.** Why hasn't Gao Wenzhong told his sister how he feels about Bai Ying'ai?

_____

**2.** Do any of Gao Wenzhong's friends know for sure how Gao Wenzhong feels about Bai Ying'ai? Why or why not?

_____

**3.** What is Gao Wenzhong's "dream girl" like?

_____

**4.** Was Gao Xiaoyin optimistic at first about her brother's chances of meeting his "dream girl"? Why or why not?

_____

**5.** Does Gao Xiaoyin now know who Gao Wenzhong's dream girl is? Who is she?

_____

**D.** Look at the listing and answer the following questions.

中影电影院
周二全天半价；周一至五 12:00 前半价
上映影片：
《危情24小时》9:00 10:55 12:50
14:45 16:40 18:35
《功夫熊猫》9:00 11:50 12:40
13:40 15:30 16:20 17:20 19:10
20:00 20:30 21:00
《精舞门》10:50 14:30 18:10

**1.** What's the name of this movie theater? _____

**2.** How many movies are currently playing in this theater? _____

**3.** How many showings are there daily for the first movie? _____

**4.** Can you get a half-price ticket if you go to see a movie in this theater on a Monday morning? _____

## IV. Writing Exercises

**A.** Answer the following questions based on your own situation.

1. A: 你去过哪些城市？

   B: _____

   A: 你对哪一个城市的印象最糟糕？

   B: _____

2. A: 你去过哪些学校？

   B: _____

   A: 你对哪一个学校的印象最好？

   B: _____

3. A: 你看过中国电影吗？

   B: _____

   A: 你对中国电影的印象怎么样？

   B: _____

**B.** Are the following items available for purchase in the place where you live?

EXAMPLE: 中国音乐

A: <u>这个城市买得到买不到中国音乐？</u>

B: <u>这个城市买得到中国音乐。/</u>

<u>这个城市买不到中国音乐。</u>

1. 中国影碟 (movie DVDs)

   **A:** _____

   **B:** _____

2. 中国地图

   **A:** _____

   **B:** _____

3. 中国绿茶

   **A:** _____

   **B:** _____

**C.** Are the following dishes available in your local restaurants?

EXAMPLE:   红烧牛肉

**A:** <u>这个城市吃得到吃不到红烧牛肉</u>？

**B:** <u>这个城市吃得到红烧牛肉。/</u>

<u>这个城市吃不到红烧牛肉。</u>

1. 凉拌黄瓜

   **A:** _____

   **B:** _____

2. 糖醋鱼

    **A:** _____

    **B:** _____

3. 家常豆腐

    **A:** _____

    **B:** _____

**D.** You are leaving for a trip tomorrow night and need to figure out whether you can finish the food in your refrigerator before you leave.

Example: 米饭 ✓

**A:** 冰箱里的米饭，明天吃得完吃不完？

**B:** （冰箱里的米饭，明天）吃得完。

1. 青菜 ✗

    **A:** _____     **B:** _____

2. 饺子 ✓

    **A:** _____     **B:** _____

3. 饮料 ✗

    **A:** _____     **B:** _____

4. 汤 ✓

    **A:** _____     **B:** _____

**E.** Translate the following exchanges into Chinese. (PRESENTATIONAL)

1. **A:** There are six pears on the table. Would you like to eat some?

   _____

   **B:** I can't eat pears. I am allergic to them.

   _____

   **C:** I can eat them. But six pears are too many. I can't eat them all.

   _____

2. **A:** I made three hundred dumplings yesterday. It took me a lot of effort to get the dumplings ready.

   _____

   **B:** How many people were making the dumplings?

   _____

   **A:** Only me, one person.

   _____

3. **A:** I have a great impression of Beijing. I would like to go there again.

   _____

   **B:** Great! I've always wanted to go to Beijing. But would we be able to get airline tickets?

   _____

   **A:** We have to hurry. Otherwise, it's possible that we won't be able to get them.

   _____

**F.** Provide a brief history of your friendship with someone, including who your friend is, when and where you met, how long you have known each other, when you became friends, what your friend does well, what attributes your friend has, what he/she looks like, what you have in common, what you often do together, etc. (PRESENTATIONAL)

## Dialogue II: Turning Down an Invitation

**PART TWO**

### I. Listening Comprehension

#### A. Textbook Dialogue (True/False) (INTERPRETIVE)

( ) **1.** Li You recognizes the caller's voice right away.

( ) **2.** Li You is not happy to get the call.

( ) **3.** Li You has never met the caller before.

( ) **4.** The caller wants to ask Li You to go out dancing with him.

( ) **5.** Li You tries to turn the caller down without directly saying so.

#### B. Workbook Telephone Message (INTERPRETIVE/PRESENTATIONAL)

You accidentally erased a phone message for your roommate. Reconstruct the message from memory and leave a written note in Chinese for your roommate. Take care to note the following information:

Roommate's name      Caller's name
Purpose of the call      Time of the event
Place of the event      Special request

Written message:

_____

_____

_____

_____

#### C. Listening Rejoinder (INTERPERSONAL)

In this section, you will hear two speakers talking. After hearing the first speaker, select the best from the four possible responses given by the second speaker.

_____

## II. Speaking Exercises

**A.** Answer the questions in Chinese based on the Textbook Dialogue. (INTERPRETIVE/PRESENTATIONAL)

1.  According to the caller, when, where, and how did he meet Li You?
2.  How did he get Li You's phone number?
3.  What was the purpose of his phone call?
4.  What is Li You planning to do over the next three weekends?
5.  How did Li You end the conversation?

**B.** With a partner, do a role play. One person should invite the other person to do something with him/her. The second person should come up with different reasons to turn down the invitation. Both parties should be persistent but polite. (INTERPERSONAL)

## III. Reading Comprehension (INTERPRETIVE)

### A. Building Words

If you combine the *wèn* in *wèntí* with the *hào* in *hàomǎ*, you have *wènhào*, as seen in #1 below. Can you guess what the word *wènhào* means? Complete this section by providing the characters, the *pinyin*, and the English equivalent of each new word formed this way. You may consult a dictionary if necessary.

|  | | new word | *pinyin* | English |
|---|---|---|---|---|
| 1. | "问题" 的 "问" + "号码" 的 "号" → 问+号 → | _____ | _____ | _____ |
| 2. | "搬出去" 的 "搬" + "我家" 的 "家" → 搬+家 → | _____ | _____ | _____ |
| 3. | "吃药" 的 "药" + "房间" 的 "房" → 药+房 → | _____ | _____ | _____ |
| 4. | "旅行" 的 "旅" + "图书馆" 的 "馆" → 旅+馆 → | _____ | _____ | _____ |
| 5. | "水电" 的 "电" + "红绿灯" 的 "灯" → 电+灯 → | _____ | _____ | _____ |

**B.** Read the following passage and answer the questions.

李友：王朋，今天晚上想不想跟我去看电影？我请客。

王朋：看电影？

李友：对，很好看的电影，很多人想看，票我已经买好了。

王朋：你没有车，票是怎么买的？

李友：是刚才坐公共汽车去买的。我昨天考试考得不错，我们好好儿玩儿玩儿吧。

王朋：可是我今天还没打球呢。

李友：我知道你今天晚上想打球，明天再打吧。

王朋：好，没问题，我和你去看电影。几点？

李友：八点⋯还是八点一刻？让我看看电影票⋯糟糕，我把电影票忘在公共汽车上了！

Questions (True/False)

( ) **1.** Li You wants to go see a movie because she did well on her exam.

( ) **2.** Wang Peng accepts the invitation promptly.

( ) **3.** Wang Peng had previously planned to play ball this evening.

( ) **4.** We can assume that the movie theater will be half empty this evening.

( ) **5.** It is not clear from the tickets whether the movie starts at 8:00 or 8:15.

( ) **6.** Li You says that she found the movie tickets on the bus.

**C.** Read the following dialogue and answer the questions.

高文中：哎，李友，好久不见。明天有一个音乐会，我买了两张票。一起去听，好吗？

李友：　你真客气，可是，对不起，我明天晚上得整理房间，把我的新买的冰箱搬进来。你还是跟白英爱去吧。

高文中：你不是很喜欢音乐吗？上个月学校开音乐会，你早上七点钟就去买票，费了很大力气才买到，对不对？

李友：　对，我很喜欢听音乐，可是我明天没空儿。

高文中：哎，告诉你吧，李友，这两张票是我帮王朋买的。怎么样，明天晚上不想打扫房间了吧？

Questions (True/False)

(　)1. 李友说明天晚上的音乐会没有意思。

(　)2. 王朋找高文中帮他和李友买两张票，可是没有告诉李友。

(　)3. 高文中今天早上七点就去买票了。

(　)4. 李友说她刚买了一个冰箱，可是冰箱现在不在她的房间里。

(　)5. 李友上个月去听学校的音乐会了。

(　)6. 上个月学校开音乐会，很多人不想去。

(　)7. 高文中觉得李友明天晚上不会在家打扫房间，她会跟王朋去听音乐会。

**D.** What does the store sell? Please list three items.

_____

_____

_____

# IV. Writing Exercises

## A. Building Characters

Form a character by fitting the given components together as indicated. Then provide a word or phrase in which that character appears.

EXAMPLE: 上边一个 "田"，下边一个 "力气" 的 "力" 是
<u>"男朋友"</u> 的 <u>"男"</u>。

1. 左边一个人字旁，右边一个 "两个" 的 "两"
   是_____ 的_____。

2. 左边一个 "讠"，右边一个 "自己" 的 "己"
   是_____ 的_____。

3. 左边一个 "走"，右边一个 "自己" 的 "己"
   是_____的_____。

4. 左边一个 "石"，右边一个 "马" 是_____
   的_____。

5. 上边一个 "生日" 的 "日"，下边一个 "医生"
   的 "生" 是_____的_____。

**B.** Answer the following questions based on your own situation.

1. **A:** 你记得不记得你上个星期五吃了些什么东西？

   **B:** _____ 。

2. **A:** 你想得起来想不起来你中学英文老师叫什么名字？

   **B:** _____ 。

3. **A:** 你知道不知道你爸爸、妈妈的手机号码？

   **B:** _____ 。

**C.** An animal obedience trainer is going to China to help Chinese clients train their dogs. The dogs there only understand Chinese. The trainer needs your help to learn some Chinese before his trip. Write down the proper commands in Chinese based on each picture.

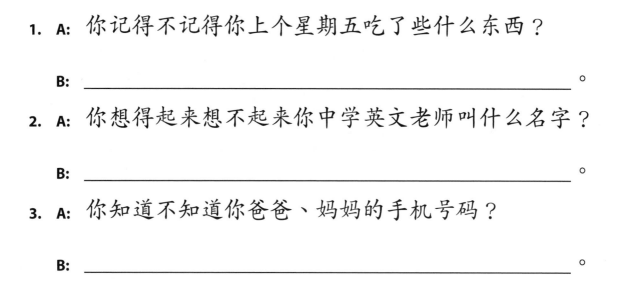

1. _____  2. _____  3. _____  4. _____

5. _____  6. _____  7. _____  8. _____

**D.** Instruct the movers to move the furniture out of the room based on the illustrations.

EXAMPLE:

→ <u>请把椅子(yǐzi)搬出房间去。/请把椅子(yǐzi)从房间搬出去。</u>

1.  → _____

2. → _____

3. → _____

**E.** Translate the following into Chinese. (PRESENTATIONAL)

1.  **A:**  When did you move out of the dorm?

    _____

    **B:**  I moved out in February.

    _____

2.  **A:**  Who's the woman sitting next to Little Wang? I can't recall.

    _____

    **B:**  I don't know her. I have never met her before.

    _____

3.  **A:**  I am going to be traveling for a year. Please remember to clean the house once a week.

    _____

    **B:**  No problem. I won't forget. Have fun. Call my cell phone if you need anything.

    _____

**F.** List three lines that you could use if you need to end a phone conversation without hurting the other person's feelings.

1.  _____

2.  _____

3.  _____

**G.** List three ways to decline a date indirectly and politely.

1. _____

2. _____

3. _____

**H.** Describe your perfect date, including the time, the location, and the activity. (PRESENTATIONAL)

## I. Storytelling (PRESENTATIONAL)

Write a story in Chinese based on the four cartoons below. Make sure that your story has a beginning, middle and end. Also make sure that the transition from one picture to the next is smooth and logical.

**1**

**2**

**3**

**4**

# LESSON 17   Renting an Apartment
## 第十七课 租房子

**17**

## PART ONE   Narrative: Finding a Better Place

### I. Listening Comprehension

**A. Textbook Narrative** (Multiple Choice) (INTERPRETIVE)

( ) **1.** How long has Wang Peng been living in his dorm?

     **a.** two weeks

     **b.** two years

     **c.** two semesters

     **d.** two months

( ) **2.** One thing about his current dorm that does *not* bother Wang Peng is its

     **a.** cost

     **b.** size

     **c.** noise

     **d.** location

( ) **3.** How long has Wang Peng been looking for an apartment?

     **a.** about a week

     **b.** about a month

     **c.** about a year

     **d.** about a semester

( ) **4.** How many rooms does the apartment have?

     **a.** three

     **b.** five

     **c.** four

     **d.** two

## B. Workbook Narrative (INTERPRETIVE/INTERPERSONAL)

When Wang Peng returned to the dorm room, he found a new message on his answering machine. Listen to the message and answer the questions.

Questions (True/False)

( )  **1.**  The speaker is probably a friend of Wang Peng's.

( )  **2.**  The speaker thinks that he and Wang Peng would be good roommates.

( )  **3.**  The speaker would like to move off campus.

( )  **4.**  The speaker is trying to persuade Wang Peng to move into a different dorm.

( )  **5.**  The speaker thinks it's great to be able to cook for oneself.

Reply to the caller by email on Wang Peng's behalf:

_____

_____

_____

## C. Listening Rejoinder (INTERPERSONAL)

In this section, you will hear two speakers talking. After hearing the first speaker, select the best from the four possible responses given by the second speaker.

_____

# II. Speaking Exercises (INTERPRETIVE/PRESENTATIONAL)

**A.** Answer the questions in Chinese based on the Textbook Narrative.

1. Why did Wang Peng want to move out of his dormitory?

2. How long has he been looking for an apartment?

3. How far away from school was the apartment listed in the advertisement he saw?

4. What information did the ad include in addition to the apartment's location?

**B.** Ask your partner where he/she lives, how far it is away from school, whether he/she likes his/her current place, and why or why not. (INTERPERSONAL)

**C.** This is Little Xia's place. With a partner, talk about the rooms in the apartment and the furniture in each room. (INTERPERSONAL)

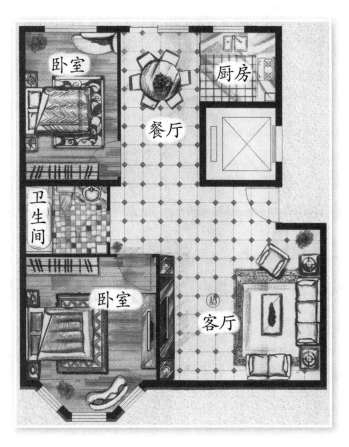

## III. Reading Comprehension (INTERPRETIVE)

### A. Building Words

If you combine the *wǎn* in *wǎnshang* with the *bào* in *bàozhǐ*, you have *wǎnbào*, as seen in #1 below. Can you guess what the word *wǎnbào* means? Complete this section by providing the characters, the *pinyin*, and the English equivalent of each new word formed this way. You may consult a dictionary if necessary.

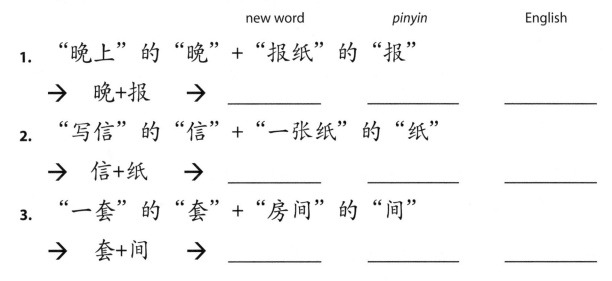

|  | new word | *pinyin* | English |
|---|---|---|---|

1. "晚上" 的 "晚" + "报纸" 的 "报"

   → 晚+报  → _____  _____  _____

2. "写信" 的 "信" + "一张纸" 的 "纸"

   → 信+纸  → _____  _____  _____

3. "一套" 的 "套" + "房间" 的 "间"

   → 套+间  → _____  _____  _____

4. "卫生间"的"卫生" + "一张纸"的"纸"

   → 卫生+纸 → _____    _____    _____

5. "厨房"的"厨" + "家具"的"具"

   → 厨+具 → _____    _____    _____

**B.** Read the following passage and answer the questions.

小马在学生宿舍住了两个学期了。因为他的房间很小，放不下两张床，所以他一个人住一个房间。宿舍里有餐厅、图书室、电脑室，还有洗衣房，非常方便。小马不太会做饭，很喜欢认识新朋友，所以他觉得住宿舍对他很合适。他听说在校外租房子比住宿舍便宜，但是得跟别人一起住，还得自己做饭，所以他现在还不知道他下个学期要不要搬出去住。

Questions (True/False)

( ) 1. 小马是两个学期以前搬进学生宿舍的。

( ) 2. 虽然房间里有两张床，可是没有别人住在小马的房间里。

( ) 3. 小马想用电脑的时候，得去学校的电脑中心。

( ) 4. 小马觉得自己做饭没有在餐厅吃饭方便。

( ) 5. 住学校宿舍虽然比住在学校外边贵，可是很方便。

( ) 6. 小马还不清楚他下个学期要住在哪儿。

**C.** Read the following passage and answer the questions.

我是今年寒假搬进我现在住的公寓的。公寓离学校很近，开车只要五分钟，买东西也很方便。虽然卧室不太大，可是厨房和客厅都很漂亮，而且家具都是新的，每个月只要五百块钱。公寓这么好，怎么这么便宜呢？我想这个问题想了三个月，上个星期才听说很多住过这个公寓的人都生病，而且如果住的时间长，病就会越来越重，不过一搬出这个公寓，他们的病就好了，所以这儿的房租一定得便宜，要不然没有人住。我应该怎么办呢？虽然现在我的身体很健康，可是我得好好儿想想，要不要准备搬家呢？

Questions (True/False)

( ) **1.** The narrator's apartment is inexpensive and conveniently located.

( ) **2.** All of the rooms in the apartment are spacious and beautifully furnished.

( ) **3.** Similar apartments elsewhere in this city are considerably more expensive.

( ) **4.** Before the narrator moved into the apartment, he talked to many former tenants of this apartment building.

Questions (Multiple Choice)

( ) **5.** What happened to many of the people who once lived in this apartment building?

    **a.** They couldn't find doctors when they got sick.

    **b.** They couldn't move out when they got sick.

    **c.** Their health was temporarily affected.

    **d.** Their health was permanently affected.

( ) **6.** The narrator didn't find out the truth behind the low rent until _____.

    **a.** winter break

    **b.** last week

    **c.** three months ago

    **d.** March

( ) **7.** The narrator sounds very _____ at the end of the passage.

    **a.** bitter

    **b.** ill

    **c.** indifferent

    **d.** hesitant

**D.** Look at the floor plan and answer the following questions.

1. 请用英文写出这个公寓有什么房间：

   _____

2. "主卧室"英文是 _____

# IV. Writing Exercises

**A.** What rooms does your apartment, house, or dorm have? List them in Chinese.

_____ _____

_____ _____

_____ _____

_____ _____

...

**B.** Answer the following questions about your living quarters in Chinese.

1. 你住的地方是宿舍、房子、还是公寓？吵不吵？
2. 你自己一个人住还是跟别人一起住？
3. 你住的地方带不带家具？
4. 有没有自己的厕所、卫生间？
5. 有没有厨房？可以做饭吗？
6. 上学、坐车、买东西方便不方便？
7. 附近有什么饭馆、商店？
8. 卧室大不大？放得下放不下一个大电视？
9. 你在现在住的地方住了多长时间了？
10. 下个学期你准备搬家吗？为什么？

**C.** Answer the following questions about your commute in Chinese.

1. 你今天是怎么去学校的？走路、开车、还是坐车？

2. 你今天是什么时候到学校的？

3. 你今天是自己一个人还是跟同学一起去学校的？

4. 你住的地方离学校远不远？走路走多长时间？/开车开多长时间？/坐公共汽车坐多长时间？

**D.** The main cast members of *Integrated Chinese* are all learning something. Ask and answer questions about their new endeavors based on the information given.

EXAMPLE:          cooking          three months

A: <u>王朋学做饭学了多长时间了？</u>

B: <u>王朋学做饭学了三个月了。</u>

1.          driving          one month

A: _____

B: _____

2.          English          half a year

A: _____

B: _____

3.          ice skating          two weeks

A: _____

B: _____

4.          computer          five days

A: _____

B: _____

**E.** Describe how much you can eat.

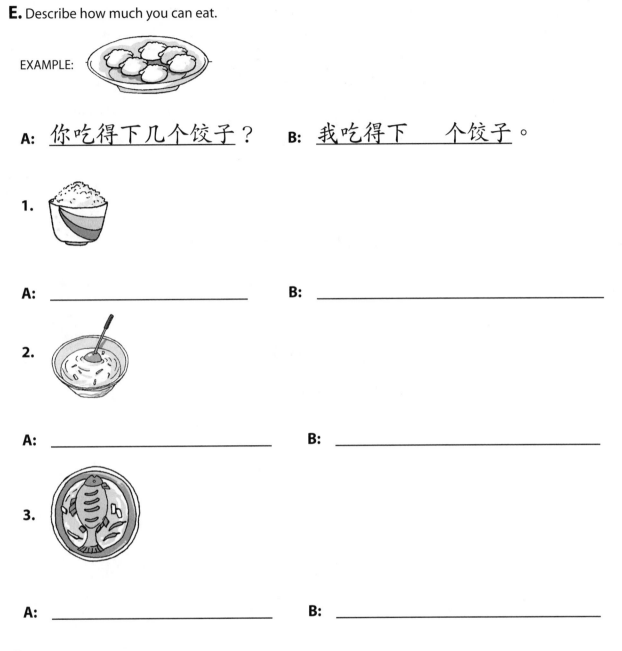

EXAMPLE:

**A:** 你吃得下几个饺子？    **B:** 我吃得下　　个饺子。

**1.**

**A:** _____    **B:** _____

**2.**

**A:** _____    **B:** _____

**3.**

**A:** _____    **B:** _____

**F.** Translate the following into Chinese. (PRESENTATIONAL)

**1. A:** My apartment is very big. There's enough room for four people.

_____

**B:** My room is small; it can't even fit a big bed.

_____

**2.   A:**   The place where I live is close to the stores. It's convenient to go shopping.

_____

**B:**   Is that right? How long does it take to walk to the stores?

_____

**A:**   It only takes three minutes to walk there.

_____

**3.   A:**   You've been living here for a little over a month. How do you feel?

_____

**B:**   I would like to move out.

_____

**A:**   What's the matter?

_____

**B:**   It's too noisy. I can't get a good night's sleep.

_____

# Dialogue: Calling about an Apartment for Rent

**PART TWO**

## I. Listening Comprehension

### A. Textbook Dialogue (True/False) (INTERPRETIVE)

( ) **1.** There isn't any furniture in the living room.

( ) **2.** Wang Peng thinks the apartment is a little expensive.

( ) **3.** There do not seem to be any chairs in the bedroom.

( ) **4.** Wang Peng will most likely study in the living room.

( ) **5.** Wang Peng won't have to pay for utilities.

( ) **6.** Wang Peng's first payment will be $1,600.

### B. Workbook Narrative (Multiple Choice) (INTERPRETIVE)

( ) **1.** Little Huang's apartment is not very

    **a.** expensive.

    **b.** convenient.

    **c.** noisy.

    **d.** large.

( ) **2.** Little Huang probably has a

    **a.** three-room apartment.

    **b.** studio apartment.

    **c.** four-room apartment.

    **d.** two-room apartment.

( ) **3.** Little Huang doesn't have a

    **a.** bed.

    **b.** desk.

    **c.** chair.

    **d.** bookcase.

( ) **4.** Little Huang wishes his apartment were less

    **a.** expensive.

    **b.** noisy.

    **c.** cramped.

    **d.** distant from work.

### C. Workbook Dialogue (True/False) (INTERPRETIVE)

Questions (True/False)

( ) **1.** The bedroom is the best room in the apartment.

( ) **2.** The man likes the bedroom, because he will spend most of his time in that room.

( ) **3.** The room where the man sleeps is well furnished.

( ) **4.** We can assume that nobody will be using the desk.

( ) **5.** Pets are allowed in this apartment building.

( ) **6.** Meimei likes to eat takeout food.

( ) **7.** Meimei is like a faithful servant to the man.

### D. Listening Rejoinder (INTERPERSONAL)

In this section, you will hear two speakers talking. After hearing the first speaker, select the best from the four possible responses given by the second speaker.

_____

# II. Speaking Exercises

**A.** Answer the questions in Chinese based on the Textbook Dialogue. (INTERPRETIVE/PRESENTATIONAL)

1.  What furniture is provided with the apartment?
2.  How much is the rent per month?
3.  What kind of discount did the landlady offer Wang Peng?
4.  How much is the deposit?
5.  Do you think that Wang Peng has ever had pets? Why or why not?

**B.** Do a role play with a partner. You call your partner (a landlord) and ask about an apartment he/she has for rent. Make sure you get all the details about the apartment, such as its distance from school, the number of rooms, furniture, rent, utilities, deposit, policy on pets, etc. Set up an appointment to see the apartment in person. (INTERPERSONAL)

**C.** Describe your room, apartment, or your parents' house based on a photo or drawing. You can mention the number of rooms, its location and environment, its distance from school, furniture, etc. (PRESENTATIONAL)

# III. Reading Comprehension (INTERPRETIVE)

## A. Building Words

If you combine the *lěng* in *hěn lěng* with the *jìng* in *ānjìng*, you have *lěngjìng*, as seen in #1 below. Can you guess what the word *lěngjìng* means? Complete this section by providing the characters, the *pinyin*, and the English equivalent of each new word formed this way. You may consult a dictionary if necessary.

|     |     | new word | *pinyin* | English |
|-----|-----|----------|----------|---------|
| 1. | "很冷" 的 "冷" ＋ "安静" 的 "静" ➡ 冷+静 ➡ | _____ | _____ | _____ |
| 2. | "安静" 的 "静" ＋ "水电" 的 "电" ➡ 静+电 ➡ | _____ | _____ | _____ |
| 3. | "报纸" 的 "纸" ＋ "人民币" 的 "币" ➡ 纸+币 ➡ | _____ | _____ | _____ |
| 4. | "学习" 的 "学" ＋ "水电费" 的 "费" ➡ 学+费 ➡ | _____ | _____ | _____ |
| 5. | "出租" 的 "租" ＋ "押金" 的 "金" ➡ 租+金 ➡ | _____ | _____ | _____ |

**B.** Read the following passage and answer the questions.

　　小张在学校宿舍住了两年了，最近才搬出来，在学校附近租了一套公寓。公寓里什么家具都没有。朋友们告诉小张什么都不用买。他们有很多家具，送给了小张一个书桌，两个书架和一张床。那张床特别漂亮，哪个家具店都买不到。他们还说，要是小张还要别的东西，什么时候给他们打电话都可以。

Questions (True/False)

( )**1.** Little Zhang has lived in the apartment for two years.

( )**2.** The apartment is not furnished.

( )**3.** His friends want to know what furniture Little Zhang wants to buy.

( )**4.** Little Zhang wonders what furniture store he should visit to find a beautiful bed.

( )**5.** Little Zhang will not have to spend any money on furniture.

( )**6.** His friends want to know when Little Zhang will call them.

**C.** Read the following passage and answer the questions.

　　小黄上个月在学校附近找了一套小公寓，一房一厅，还带家具。房租每个月只要五百二十块。小黄觉得比住在学校宿舍便宜多了，所以就搬进去了。可是他搬进去以后才知道，他每个月得付九十块钱的水电费。小黄觉得太贵了。昨天他又找到了一套房子，虽然离学校有一点儿远，可是很安静，房租每个月五百四十块，不用付水电费。小黄对那套公寓很有兴趣，想下个星期搬进去。因为他在现在的公寓只住了一个月，所以他得多付一个月的房租才能搬出去。

Questions (True/False)

( )**1.** Little Huang has lived in his current apartment for one semester.

( )**2.** Little Huang thought his current apartment was inexpensive when he moved in.

( )**3.** The student dorm on campus costs $520 per month.

( )**4.** Little Huang has to pay at least $610 a month for his current apartment.

( )**5.** Little Huang's current apartment is far away from campus.

( )**6.** After he moves into the new apartment, he will pay only $540 per month.

( )**7.** Little Huang's new apartment is quiet but relatively far from campus.

( )**8.** When he moves out of his current apartment, he will have to pay an extra $90.

**D.** Draw a picture based on the reading.

　　李先生的家楼下有一个客厅，一个厕所，一个厨房。客厅里的家具不多，就一个沙发，一个咖啡桌。你看，李先生正坐在沙发上看报纸呢！厨房里有一张饭桌和四把椅子。楼上有两个卧室，一个卫生间。每个卧室都有一张床，李太太正在打扫整理右边的卧室！左边的卧室是谁的呢？我想起来了，是他们儿子的房间。他怎么躺在床上呢？糟糕，他对房子附近的花过敏，眼睛很不舒服！…你看，他们家的狗小白正在房子外边玩呢。小白眼睛大大的，嘴也大大的，非常可爱。

**E.** Here are two "house for rent" ads. Which of the two would you pick? Why?

| 房屋租售 | 房屋出租 | 房屋出租 |
|---|---|---|
| | 三房两厅 | $180-$350 |
| | 两个厕所 | |
| | 有冰箱，洗衣机 | 及电视CABLE，近公车站 |
| | 月租：$1375 | 有意者请电:206- |
| | 有意请电:425-754- | 682-XXXX |
| | XXXX | |

---

# IV. Writing Exercises

## A. Building Characters

Form a character by fitting the given components together as indicated. Then provide a word or phrase in which that character appears.

EXAMPLE: 上边一个"田"，下边一个"力气"的"力"是
"<u>男朋友</u>"的"<u>男</u>"。

1. 左边一个"口"，右边一个"多少"的"少"是
_____的_____。

2. 左边一个"禾"，右边一个"而且"的"且"是
_____的_____。

3. 左边一个人字旁，右边一个"寸"是_____的
_____。

4. 左边一个三点水，右边一个"多少"的"少"是
_____的_____。

5. 上边一个"加州"的"加"，下边一个"木"是
_____的_____。

**B.** List the pieces of furniture in the place where you currently live.

_____    _____    _____    _____

...

**C.** Search online to answer the following questions. Don't forget to cite the website you used and provide the date of your search.

1. 一百元美元能换多少人民币？→ _____

2. 一百元人民币能换多少美元？→ _____

网站：_____

日期：_____

**D.** Rewrite the following sentences.

EXAMPLE: 小夏不认识小王，小白，小张，小高…。

→小夏谁都/也不认识。

1. 老师上午、中午、下午、晚上都没空。

→_____

2. 这个房间没有桌子、椅子、床…。

→_____

3. 我弟弟喝茶、喝水、喝可乐、喝咖啡、也喝果汁。

→_____

4. 李老师对小王的印象不好，对小张、小白、小高的印象也不好。

→_____

**E.** 如果你想租房子，租房子以前，你会问房东哪些问题？

1. _____ ?

2. _____ ?

3. _____ ?

4. _____ ?

5. _____ ?

6. _____ ?

7. _____ ?

8. _____ ?

9. _____ ?

10. _____ ?

**F.** 你的朋友正想租房子，下边是报纸上的一个出租广告，你觉得对你的朋友很合适。可是你的朋友看不懂英文，请你用中文告诉他广告上说些什么。(PRESENTATIONAL)

```
Apt for Rent

3br, 1LR, 2ba, furnished
quiet

walk to Univ
close to bus stop, shopping, and park
$965 a month, utilities included
no pets allowed

555-5555
```

**G.** Translate the following into Chinese. (PRESENTATIONAL)

**1.  A:** This living room is so clean.

_____

**B:** It's too clean! It has nothing [in it], not even a piece of furniture or a piece of paper.

_____

**2.  A:** What are you interested in?

_____

**B:** I am interested in keeping pets.

_____

**3.** I've been living with my friend for more than two years. Our apartment is furnished and very close to school, the park, and the bus stop. The rent is less expensive than living in the dorm. I like where I live. My friend is also very nice to me. He cleans the house once a week and often hosts dance parties. Even my mother likes the place I live in. But I may have to move out next semester. It's not because it's so noisy that I cannot sleep well, and it's not because I am allergic to my friend's dog. It's because my friend's cousin is moving in and the place is too small to house three people. It's difficult to find a suitable and affordable apartment. I'm thinking I could ask my friend if he would like to find a house that's a little bigger.

_____

_____

_____

_____

_____

_____

_____

**H.** List the things that you like and dislike about the place you currently live in.

喜欢                                不喜欢

1. _____      1. _____

2. _____      2. _____

3. _____      3. _____

• • •                            • • •

**I.** Based on the lists in the previous exercise, describe your ideal living quarters. (PRESENTATIONAL)

## J. Storytelling (PRESENTATIONAL)

Write a story based on the four cartoons below. Make sure that your story has a beginning, middle and end. Also make sure that the transition from one picture to the next is smooth and logical.

1
2
3
4

# 18

## LESSON 18  Sports
第十八课 运动

| PART ONE | Dialogue I: My Gut Keeps Getting Bigger and Bigger! |

## I. Listening Comprehension

### A. Textbook Dialogue (True/False) (INTERPRETIVE)

( ) **1.** Wang Peng says he has been putting on weight.

( ) **2.** Gao Wenzhong wants to start exercising right away.

( ) **3.** Gao Wenzhong hasn't exercised in two years.

( ) **4.** Wang Peng suggests that Gao Wenzhong take up martial arts.

( ) **5.** Gao Wenzhong thinks playing basketball is too expensive.

### B. Workbook Telephone Message (Multiple Choice) (INTERPRETIVE)

Bai Ying'ai called Gao Wenzhong, but he was not in, so she left him a message. Answer the following questions after you listen to the message.

( ) **1.** Bai Ying'ai called Gao Wenzhong to ask him to

    **a.** attend her birthday party.

    **b.** play tennis.

    **c.** have breakfast.

    **d.** meet her classmate.

( ) **2.** Bai Ying'ai suggests that Gao Wenzhong should

    **a.** buy a tennis racket.

    **b.** buy some tennis balls.

    **c.** hire a tennis coach.

    **d.** get a pair of tennis shoes.

( )  **3.** Who else may be there?

    **a.** Bai Ying'ai's father.

    **b.** Bai Ying'ai's classmate.

    **c.** Bai Ying'ai's pal Wang Peng.

    **d.** Bai Ying'ai's teacher.

( )  **4.** Bai Ying'ai thinks that Gao Wenzhong may not want to go because

    **a.** Gao Wenzhong feels tennis shoes are too expensive.

    **b.** Gao Wenzhong doesn't eat breakfast.

    **c.** Gao Wenzhong can't get up early.

    **d.** Gao Wenzhong isn't enthusiastic about playing sports.

## C. Listening Rejoinder (INTERPERSONAL)

In this section, you will hear two speakers talking. After hearing the first speaker, select the best from the four possible responses given by the second speaker.

_____

# II. Speaking Exercises

**A.** Answer the questions in Chinese based on the Textbook Dialogue. (INTERPRETIVE/PRESENTATIONAL)

1. According to Wang Peng, why has Gao Wenzhong gained weight?
2. How often and for how long does Wang Peng recommend Gao Wenzhong should exercise?
3. How long has it been since Gao Wenzhong exercised?
4. What sports does Wang Peng recommend?
5. What excuse does Gao Wenzhong give for disliking jogging?
6. Why does Wang Peng recommend swimming?
7. What is Wang Peng's conclusion?

**B.** Ask your partner if he/she exercises, how often, what kind of exercise he/she does, and why he/she likes that kind of exercise. (INTERPERSONAL)

## III. Reading Comprehension (INTERPRETIVE)

### A. Building Words

If you combine the *pǎo* in *pǎo bù* with the *chē* in *qìchē*, you have *pǎochē*, as seen in #1 below. Can you guess what the word *pǎochē* means? Complete this section by providing the characters, the *pinyin*, and the English equivalent of each new word formed this way. You may consult a dictionary if necessary.

|  | new word | *pinyin* | English |
|---|---|---|---|
| **1.** "跑步"的"跑" + "汽车"的"车" <br> → 跑+车 → | _____ | _____ | _____ |
| **2.** "上网"的"网" + "人民"的"民" <br> → 网+民 → | _____ | _____ | _____ |
| **3.** "一把花"的"花" + "篮球"的"篮" <br> → 花+篮 → | _____ | _____ | _____ |
| **4.** "游泳"的"泳" + "衣服"的"衣" <br> → 泳+衣 → | _____ | _____ | _____ |
| **5.** "危险"的"危" + "楼下"的"楼" <br> → 危+楼 → | _____ | _____ | _____ |

**B.** Read the following passage and answer the questions.

　　大明是小明的哥哥，他们都喜欢运动。大明每个星期打一次篮球，有时候还跟朋友一起去打网球。要是朋友都很忙，不能去打球，大明就自己一个人去跑步。小明跟大明不一样，已经两年没有运动了，只喜欢看别人运动。他觉得球赛比什么都好看，电视里一有篮球比赛或者网球赛，小明就坐在沙发上看，有时候连饭都不想吃。大明今年三十五岁，但因为常常运动，身体好极了。小明今年只有二十五岁，可是越来越胖。大明小明两个在一起，不认识他们的人常说大明是弟弟，小明是哥哥。小明不懂为什么他和哥哥都喜欢运动，可是身体没有哥哥那么好。

Questions (True/False)

( )**1.** The older brother looks younger than the younger brother.
( )**2.** Running is Daming's favorite kind of exercise.
( )**3.** The last time Xiaoming exercised was two years ago.
( )**4.** When there is a ball game on TV, Xiaoming doesn't want to watch anything else.
( )**5.** Xiaoming has gained weight because he doesn't eat regularly.
( )**6.** Both brothers love sports, but in very different ways.

**C.** Read the following passage and answer the questions.

哥哥：你最近常常生病，身体越来越糟糕，要想身体好，
　　　就得运动。运动不必多，做一种运动就够了。

弟弟：一种运动就够了？我做过好几种运动，可是一点儿
　　　用都没有。半年前我就开始打网球了。

哥哥：网球是一种很好的运动。你现在跟谁一起打？

弟弟：我五个月没打网球了。我觉得游泳更有意思，所以
　　　打了两次网球，就去游泳了。

哥哥：游泳也不错。你现在在哪儿游泳？

弟弟：我四个月没游泳了。我游了两个多星期的泳，觉得
　　　还是打篮球方便，就开始打篮球了。

哥哥：你不说我也知道，你打了几次篮球，觉得没什么意
　　　思，好几个月没打了，对不对？我现在才知道，你
　　　的身体为什么这么不好。

1.  What was the older brother's initial advice to the younger brother on losing weight?

    _____

2.  What sports did the younger brother try recently?

    _____

3.  How long did the younger brother play tennis?

    _____

4.  When did the younger brother stop going swimming?

    _____

5.  Why do you think none of the sports worked for the younger brother?

    _____

6.  Why did the older brother change his estimate of the younger brother's chances of getting healthy?

    _____

**D.** Answer the following question based on the TV guide provided.

**BTV6**
11:15 篮球风云
13:15 奥运故事 365
16:00 NBA 精彩回放
21:25 直播:天天体育

What time(s) can you definitely watch basketball programming? _____

# IV. Writing Exercises

**A.** Answer the following questions and explain your opinions.

1.  什么运动很危险?

    → _____

2. 什么运动很简单？

→_____

3. 什么运动很麻烦？

→_____

4. 什么运动得花很多时间？

→_____

5. 什么运动得花很多钱？

→_____

**B.** Little Wang has been so busy studying this semester that he has neglected a lot of other things. State what he hasn't had time to do, and for how long, based on the illustrations given.

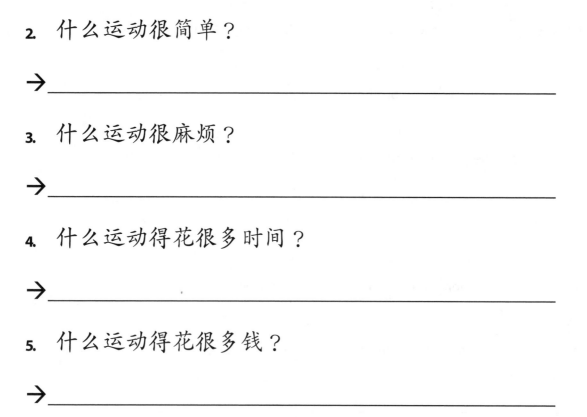

EXAMPLE:                                    ✗         two months

→小王两个月没运动了。

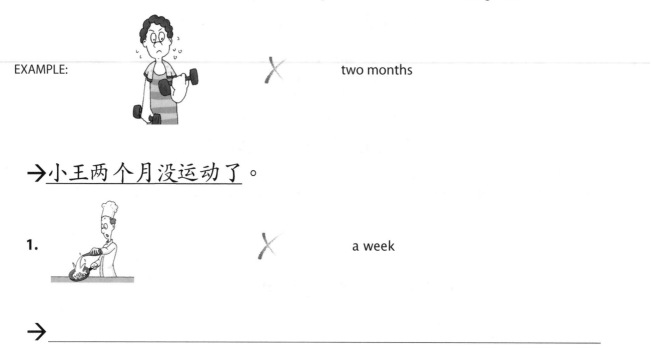

1.                                          ✗         a week

→_____

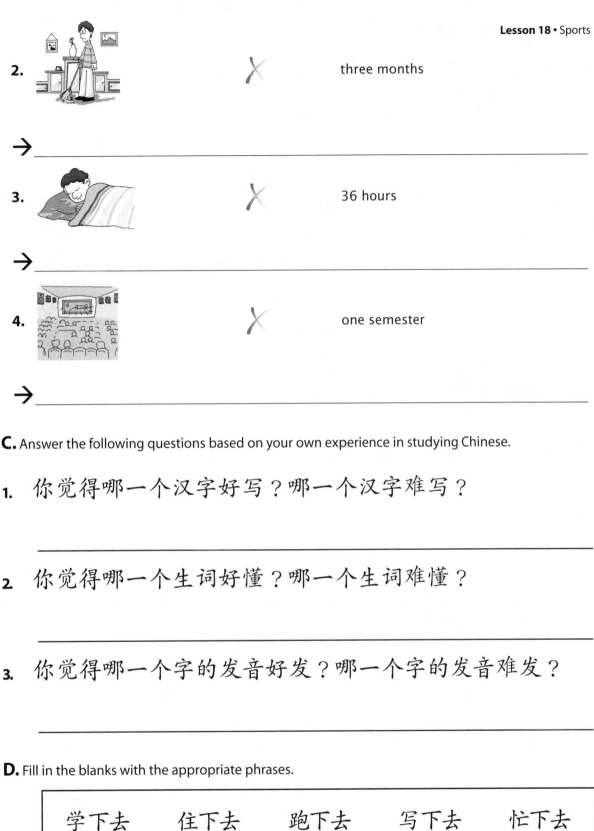

2.                              ✗              three months

→ _____

3.                              ✗              36 hours

→ _____

4.                              ✗              one semester

→ _____

**C.** Answer the following questions based on your own experience in studying Chinese.

1. 你觉得哪一个汉字好写？哪一个汉字难写？

   _____

2. 你觉得哪一个生词好懂？哪一个生词难懂？

   _____

3. 你觉得哪一个字的发音好发？哪一个字的发音难发？

   _____

**D.** Fill in the blanks with the appropriate phrases.

| 学下去 | 住下去 | 跑下去 | 写下去 | 忙下去 |
|---|---|---|---|---|

1. 这个公寓对我很合适，明年我想_____，不想搬出去。

2. 我写日记写了很多年了，还会_____。

3. 中文非常有意思，我下个学期一定_____。

**4.**　你最近忙得不能好好儿吃饭、睡觉，再这么_____，
　　　一定会生病，休息几天吧。

**E.** Translate the following into Chinese. (PRESENTATIONAL)

**1. A:** Why don't you like to swim? Are you afraid of water?

_____

**B:** Of course not. I feel it's too much trouble to go swimming.

_____

**2. A:** You studied dancing for three years. Why didn't you continue?

_____

**B:** I was too tired, and I was not willing to continue.

_____

**A:** How long has it been since you danced?

_____

**B:** It's been more than six months.

_____

**3.** I have studied Chinese for more than seven months. My teacher asked us to listen to the audio recordings for half an hour every day. But I haven't done so for more than a week. There's a test tomorrow. I'd better review thoroughly and hope that I will ace the test.

_____

_____

_____

# Dialogue II: Watching American Football

**PART TWO**

## I. Listening Comprehension

### A. Textbook Dialogue (True/False) (INTERPRETIVE)

( ) **1.** Wang Hong has watched soccer in the past.

( ) **2.** Wang Hong is not familiar with American football.

( ) **3.** Gao Xiaoyin's boyfriend loves to watch American football.

( ) **4.** Wang Hong is instantly hooked on American football.

### B. Workbook Dialogue (True/False) (INTERPRETIVE)

( ) **1.** The woman doesn't believe that Gao Wenzhong went to play tennis.

( ) **2.** Gao Wenzhong may not like playing tennis much, but he likes his tennis partner.

( ) **3.** The man gives high marks to Gao Wenzhong's positive attitude.

( ) **4.** Gao Wenzhong gave up tennis after one lesson.

( ) **5.** The woman thinks that Gao Wenzhong may well succeed in losing weight.

### C. Listening Rejoinder (INTERPERSONAL)

In this section, you will hear two speakers talking. After hearing the first speaker, select the best from the four possible responses given by the second speaker.

## II. Speaking Exercises

**A.** Answer the questions in Chinese based on the Textbook Dialogue. (INTERPRETIVE/PRESENTATIONAL)

1. How much time did Wang Hong spend watching TV and why?

2. What kind of game did Gao Xiaoyin want to watch?

3. What two differences between American football and soccer did Gao Xiaoyin mention?

4. Why did Wang Hong want to switch the TV channel?

5. Do you think that Gao Xiaoyin's boyfriend likes to watch American football? Why or why not?

**B.** Ask your partner how often he/she watches TV and whether he/she watches sports on TV. If so, which sports does he/she watch? (INTERPERSONAL)

**C.** Tell your classmates whether you like to watch American football and explain the reasons why you like or dislike watching it. (PRESENTATIONAL)

## III. Reading Comprehension (INTERPRETIVE)

### A. Building Words

If you combine the *sài* in *bǐsài* with the *pǎo* in *pǎo bù*, you have *sàipǎo*, as seen in #1 below. Can you guess what the word *sàipǎo* means? Complete this section by providing the characters, the *pinyin*, and the English equivalent of each new word formed this way. You may consult a dictionary if necessary.

|  | new word | *pinyin* | English |
|---|---|---|---|

1. "比赛"的"赛" + "跑步"的"跑"

   → 赛+跑 → _____ _____ _____

2. "比赛"的"赛" + "唱歌"的"歌"

   → 赛+歌 → _____ _____ _____

3. "水平"的"平" + "手"

   → 平+手 → _____ _____ _____

4. "天气"的"气" + "压坏"的"压"

   → 气+压 → _____ _____ _____

5. "运动"的"动" + "宠物"的"物"

   → 动+物 → _____ _____ _____

**B.** Read the following passage and answer the questions.

为了提高自己的中文水平，白先生每天下午开车到图书馆去看两个多小时的中国电影。今天吃完午饭他想去图书馆，才想起来自己的汽车刚被表弟开回家去了。他打电话请表弟把车开回来，可是表弟的太太说，车让他开到机场去了。白先生知道今天不能去图书馆了。

Questions (True/False)

( )**1.** Mr. Bai is most likely a native Chinese speaker.

( )**2.** Mr. Bai spends at least two hours in the library every day.

( )**3.** Mr. Bai's home is not within walking distance of the library.

( )**4.** Mr. Bai drove his cousin's car to the library yesterday.

( )**5.** His cousin was not home when Mr. Bai called.

( )**6.** Mr. Bai still plans on going to the library later this afternoon.

**C.** Read the passage and answer the questions.

张英和妹妹都喜欢打网球。张英每个星期六下午打两个小时的球，然后回家吃晚饭。上个星期六她没打，因为球拍被妹妹拿去了。妹妹那天要跟朋友打球，她觉得姐姐的球拍比她的好。今天又是星期六。张英告诉妈妈她晚上七点半才会回家吃晚饭，因为上个星期六她没打球，所以今天要打四个小时的球。

**1.** Why didn't Zhang Ying play tennis last Saturday?

_____

**2.** What did Zhang Ying's sister do last Saturday?

_____

**3.** When do you think Zhang Ying will start playing tennis today?

_____

**4.** Does Zhang Ying usually have dinner at 7:30 on Saturdays?

_____

**5.** How much longer than usual will Zhang Ying play tennis today?

_____

**D.** Read the passage and answer the questions.

高小音的男朋友很喜欢运动。他每天游一个小时的泳，每个星期打一次篮球。他没有踢过美式足球，可是美式足球是他最喜欢看的球赛。高小音刚从英国来美国的时候，不太懂美式足球，可是现在跟男朋友一样，都爱看美式足球，电视上一有美式足球赛他们俩就连饭也忘了吃。

Questions (True/False)

( ) **1.** Gao Xiaoyin's boyfriend is a good swimmer, good basketball player, and good football player.

( ) **2.** Gao Xiaoyin's boyfriend exercises at least seven hours every week.

( ) **3.** Gao Xiaoyin was a football fan before she came to the United States.

( ) **4.** Gao Xiaoyin felt that her boyfriend's enthusiasm for football was contagious.

( ) **5.** Before watching a football game on TV, they usually have a meal in a restaurant.

**E.** Here's a daily TV guide for the sports channels. Do you see any soccer programs? If so, please circle them.

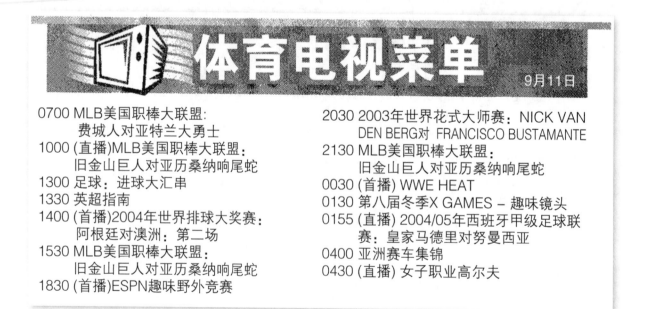

体育电视菜单  9月11日

0700 MLB美国职棒大联盟：
　　　费城人对亚特兰大勇士
1000 (直播)MLB美国职棒大联盟：
　　　旧金山巨人对亚历桑纳响尾蛇
1300 足球：进球大汇串
1330 英超指南
1400 (首播)2004年世界排球大奖赛：
　　　阿根廷对澳洲：第二场
1530 MLB美国职棒大联盟：
　　　旧金山巨人对亚历桑纳响尾蛇
1830 (首播)ESPN趣味野外竞赛

2030 2003年世界花式大师赛：NICK VAN
　　　DEN BERG对 FRANCISCO BUSTAMANTE
2130 MLB美国职棒大联盟：
　　　旧金山巨人对亚历桑纳响尾蛇
0030 (首播) WWE HEAT
0130 第八届冬季X GAMES – 趣味镜头
0155 (直播) 2004/05年西班牙甲级足球联
　　　赛：皇家马德里对努曼西亚
0400 亚洲赛车集锦
0430 (直播) 女子职业高尔夫

# IV. Writing Exercises

## A. Building Characters

Form a character by fitting the given components together as indicated. Then provide a word or phrase in which that character appears.

EXAMPLE: 左边一个"月"，右边一个"土"是__"肚子"__的

__"肚"__。

1. 左边一个"月"，右边一个"半天"的"半"

   是_____ 的_____。

2. 左边一个提手旁，右边一个"白色"的"白"

   是_____ 的_____。

3. 左边一个提手旁，右边一个"是"

   是_____的_____。

4. 左边一个足字旁，右边一个"容易"的"易"

   是_____的_____。

5. 上边一个"音乐"的"音"，下边一个"中心"的

   "心"是_____的_____。

**B.** Answer the following questions based on your own workout routine.

1. 你喜欢什么运动？

   _____

2. 你常常去什么地方运动？

   _____

3. 你一个星期/一个月运动几次？

_____

4. 你每次运动多长时间？

_____

5. 你多长时间没运动了？

_____

**C.** Answer the following questions based on your own situation.

1. 你的中文老师平常坐着上课还是站着上课？

_____

2. 你常常坐着还是躺着听音乐？

_____

3. 你觉得抱着球跑累不累？

_____

**D.** Take a look at the chart and summarize who did what for how long yesterday.

| EXAMPLE | 1. | 2. | 3. | 4. | 5. |
|---|---|---|---|---|---|
| 4:00pm–6:00pm | 7:00am–8:00am | 8:30am–12:00pm | 5:45pm–6:30pm | 10:00pm–10:15pm | entire day |

EXAMPLE:

李友昨天打扫房子打扫了两个小时/钟头。

or  李友昨天打扫了两个小时（的）房子。

1. _____

2. _____

3. _____

4. _____

5. _____

**E.** Describe the following situations based on the illustrations given.

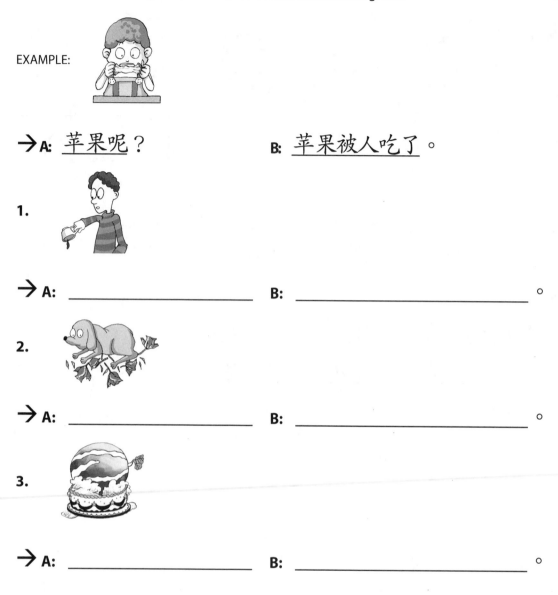

EXAMPLE:

→ A: <u>苹果呢？</u>   B: <u>苹果被人吃了</u>。

1.

→ A: _____   B: _____ 。

2.

→ A: _____   B: _____ 。

3.

→ A: _____   B: _____ 。

**F.** Translate the following into Chinese. (PRESENTATIONAL)

1. **A:** The weather is getting colder and colder. You'd better put on some more clothes. Otherwise, you may catch a cold.

   _____

   **B:** Don't worry. I am in great physical condition. I don't get sick easily.

   _____

2. **A:** How come my tennis ball is not round any more?

   _____

   **B:** I am sorry. It got crushed by the sofa.

   _____

3. **A:** Class, I have a fever. Today I have to give the lesson sitting down.

   _____

   **B:** Teacher, you should go home and rest.

   _____

4. **A:** Old Wang, do you know how to send text messages?

   _____

   **B:** I don't. I don't even know how to e-mail.

   _____

   **A:** Old Wang, you don't even have a cell phone, right?

   _____

   **B:** Right!

   _____

**G.** Design your own ideal weekly workout schedule, including types of exercise, locations, frequency, and duration of each workout. (PRESENTATIONAL)

## H. Storytelling (PRESENTATIONAL)

Write a story based on the four cartoons below. Make sure that your story has a beginning, middle, and end. Also make sure that the transition from one picture to the next is smooth and logical.

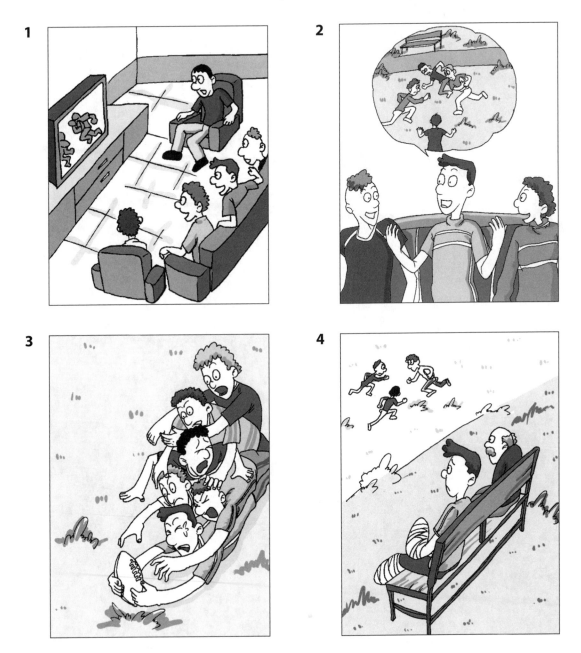

# LESSON 19   **Travel**
第十九课 旅行

19

## PART ONE   Dialogue I: Traveling to Beijing

## I. Listening Comprehension

### A. Textbook Dialogue (Multiple Choice) (INTERPRETIVE)

( )  **1.**  What does Wang Peng plan to do during the summer break?

    **a.**  apply for an internship
    **b.**  visit his parents
    **c.**  take summer classes
    **d.**  get a part-time job

( )  **2.**  At the beginning of the conversation, what summer plans did Li You have?

    **a.**  nothing definite
    **b.**  get a part-time job
    **c.**  visit her parents
    **d.**  take summer classes

( )  **3.**  Li You seems to be especially interested in Beijing's many_____.

    **a.**  good restaurants
    **b.**  important libraries
    **c.**  cultural centers
    **d.**  interesting stores

( )  **4.**  If Li You wanted to leave for Beijing today, she wouldn't have to worry about _____.

    **a.**  her passport and airline ticket
    **b.**  her passport and Chinese visa
    **c.**  her tour guide and airline ticket
    **d.**  her passport and tour guide

### B. Workbook Dialogue (True/False) (INTERPRETIVE)

( ) **1.** The woman would like to go to Northern California because she wouldn't have to speak a foreign language.

( ) **2.** The woman doesn't like to fly, and she doesn't like hot weather.

( ) **3.** The man doesn't think much of Northern California, but the woman manages to persuade him of its charms.

( ) **4.** It seems that the woman has been to Northern California before.

### C. Listening Rejoinder (INTERPERSONAL)

In this section, you will hear two speakers talking. After hearing the first speaker, select the best from the four possible responses given by the second speaker.

_____

# II. Speaking Exercises

**A.** Answer the questions in Chinese based on the Textbook Dialogue. (INTERPRETIVE/PRESENTATIONAL)

1. What will Wang Peng's classmates do over the summer?
2. What is Wang Peng's plan for the summer?
3. What did Wang Peng say about Beijing?
4. Which cities in Asia has Li You visited before?
5. What does Li You need to do in order to travel to Beijing?

**B.** Ask your partner whether he/she plans to travel, work, study, or do something else during his/her summer vacation. (INTERPERSONAL)

**C.** Search online to find out how long it takes and how much it costs to obtain a tourist visa to China. Compare notes with your partner and report to the class. (PRESENTATIONAL)

# III. Reading Comprehension (INTERPRETIVE)

## A. Building Words

If you combine the *chūn* in *chūntiān* with the *jià* in *fàng jià*, you have *chūnjià*, as seen in #1 below. Can you guess what the word *chūnjià* means? Complete this section by providing the characters, the *pinyin*, and the English equivalent of each new word formed this way. You may consult a dictionary if necessary.

|  | new word | *pinyin* | English |
|---|---|---|---|
| 1. "春天"的"春"＋"放假"的"假"<br>→ 春+假 → | _____ | _____ | _____ |
| 2. "放假"的"放"＋"担心"的"心"<br>→ 放+心 → | _____ | _____ | _____ |
| 3. "养宠物"的"养"＋"父母"的"父"<br>→ 养+父 → | _____ | _____ | _____ |
| 4. "订机票"的"订"＋"押金"的"金"<br>→ 订+金 → | _____ | _____ | _____ |
| 5. "报纸"的"报"＋"旅行社"的"社"<br>→ 报+社 → | _____ | _____ | _____ |

**B.** Read the following dialogue and answer the questions.

（还有三个星期学校就放假了。白英爱打算一放假就坐飞机回家去看爸爸妈妈，在家住三个星期，然后回学校。）

李友：　英爱，飞机票买好了吗？

白英爱：买好了。比上次回家的机票便宜不少。

李友：　是吗？你是在哪家旅行社买的？

白英爱：是高文中帮我在网上买的，他说在网上买又快、又方便、又便宜。

李友：  英爱，我觉得高文中很不错。你一点儿都不喜欢
  他吗？

白英爱：我也不知道我喜欢不喜欢他。昨天他听说我放假
  要回家，就给我打手机说要开车送我去机场。

李友：  那你跟他说什么？

白英爱：我说，要是他真的那么喜欢开车，等我回来以
  后，我跟他一起开车去加州实习吧。

李友：  哎，英爱，那他一定高兴得不得了。太好了！

Questions (True/False)

( ) **1.** Bai Ying'ai's summer break will last for only three weeks.
( ) **2.** Bai Ying'ai will leave as soon as the break starts.
( ) **3.** It was not hard for Bai Ying'ai to get an airline ticket at a good price this time.
( ) **4.** Gao Wenzhong will drive Bai Ying'ai to the airport.
( ) **5.** Bai Ying'ai probably does like Gao Wenzhong.

**C.** Read the following dialogue and answer the questions.

高小音：文中，学校要放假了，你有什么打算？上暑期班
  还是再去我们图书馆打工？

高文中：不，我要和白英爱一起去加州的一家公司实习。

高小音：是吗？

高文中：我和白英爱都没去过，可是我看过不少加州的照
  片，真是漂亮得不得了。

高小音：我去过加州好几次，就是在加州认识我男朋友
  的，所以我对加州的印象特别好。

高文中：是吗？你想不想再去一次加州？当我们的导游。

高小音：我当然想去，可是我工作太忙，也没有假。

高文中：那我和白英爱在那儿多照几张照片，用电子邮件
发给你吧。

Questions (True/False)

( ) **1.** Gao Wenzhong has never worked in Gao Xiaoyin's library.

( ) **2.** Gao Wenzhong has been to California before.

( ) **3.** California holds a special place in Gao Xiaoyin's heart.

( ) **4.** Gao Xiaoyin wishes that she could go with Gao Wenzhong.

( ) **5.** Gao Wenzhong's tour guide will help them take a lot of photos.

**D.** The following is a newspaper ad from a travel agency. Answer the questions based on the ad.

**1.** What city tour package is the ad promoting?_____

**2.** From which city will the tour depart?_____

**3.** What expenses are included in the tour package? Please list at least three.

_____

## IV. Writing Exercises

**A.** Answer the following questions based on your own situation.

1. 学校几月几号开始放暑假？

   _____

2. 暑假放多长时间？

   _____

3. 暑假你打算做什么？回家看父母、打工、出国旅行、在学校上暑期班，还是什么都不做？

   _____

**B.** See if you can figure out the English names of the following airlines.

1. 美国航空公司　　　　　　　　_____

2. 英国航空公司（英航）　　　　_____

3. 加拿大航空公司（加航）　　　_____

4. 日本航空公司（日航）　　　　_____

5. 西南航空公司　　　　　　　　_____

6. 中国东方航空公司　　　　　　_____

**c.**请把出国旅行以前得办的事，得准备或者得带的东西写出来：

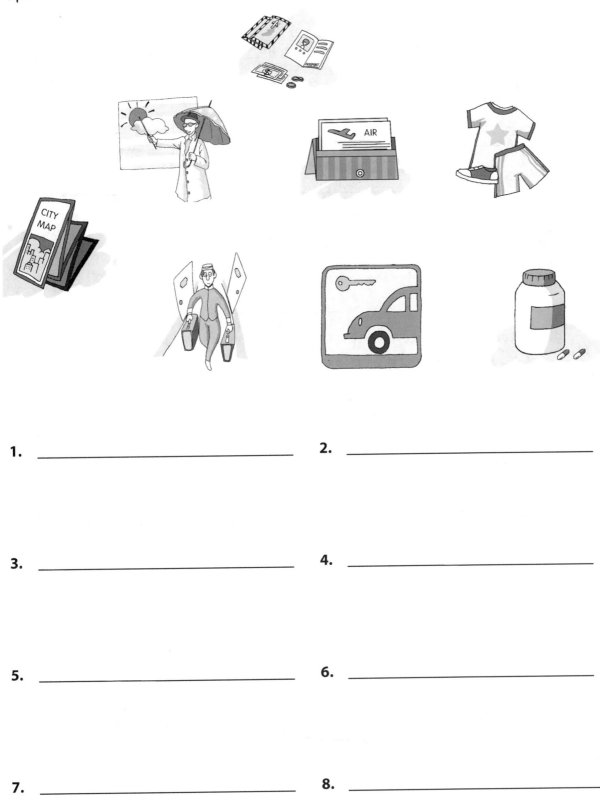

1. _____

2. _____

3. _____

4. _____

5. _____

6. _____

7. _____

8. _____

**D.** Fill in the blanks with the appropriate information.

EXAMPLE: Washington, D.C.

→Washington, D.C. <u>是美国的首都，也是美国的政治中心</u>。

1. 北京 →_____

2. 东京 →_____

3. 纽约 →_____

**E.** Translate the following into Chinese. (PRESENTATIONAL)

1. **A:** Have you ever heard of the Great Wall?

   _____

   **B:** Of course. The Great Wall is the most famous historic site in China. Everyone knows it. It's huge. Have you been to it?

   _____

   _____

   **A:** I haven't.

   _____

   **B:** I've been to the Great Wall many times. I'll take you there and be your tour guide.

   _____

**2.** How time flies! The summer break is around the corner. Some of my classmates are interning at different companies. Some are going home to work. I'll be traveling to Tokyo. Tokyo is the capital and the political and cultural center of Japan, with many famous historic sites. Good restaurants there are too many to count. I don't need a visa to go to Japan, and I have my airline ticket ready. I'm leaving tomorrow. See you next semester.

_____

_____

_____

_____

**F.** Write an essay about which cities you have visited, and which of those cities gives you the best impression. Explain why you like that city. You may include information such as the weather, the people, the shopping, the tourist sites, whether the city is a political or cultural center, etc. Alternatively, pick a city you would like to visit in the future and write about why you have a good impression of that city as a travel destination. (PRESENTATIONAL)

What kind of ads are welcome here?

**PART TWO** **Dialogue II: Planning an Itinerary**

## I. Listening Comprehension

### A. Textbook Dialogue (True/False) (INTERPRETIVE)

( ) **1.** Wang Peng and Li You will leave for Beijing in early June.

( ) **2.** Wang Peng and Li You plan to stay in Beijing for about a month.

( ) **3.** Wang Peng and Li You don't have any seat preferences for the flight to Beijing.

( ) **4.** Wang Peng asked for vegetarian meals for Li You and himself.

( ) **5.** Wang Peng decided to fly on Air China because the price is better.

### B. Workbook Narrative (True/False) (INTERPRETIVE)

( ) **1.** Little Wang doesn't like flying because of safety reasons.

( ) **2.** The cabin temperature is never comfortable enough for Little Wang.

( ) **3.** Little Wang often gets an upset stomach from eating airline food.

( ) **4.** Little Wang often misses his connections because he spends too much time in airport restaurants.

( ) **5.** Little Wang prefers to travel by car.

### C. Listening Rejoinder (INTERPERSONAL)

In this section, you will hear two speakers talking. After hearing the first speaker, select the best from the four possible responses given by the second speaker.

## II. Speaking Exercises

**A.** Answer the questions in Chinese based on the Textbook Dialogue. (INTERPRETIVE/PRESENTATIONAL)

1. When does Wang Peng plan to go back to Beijing this summer?
2. What is his strategy for deciding which airline to fly on?
3. Why did Wang Peng choose to fly on Air China?
4. Did Wang Peng ask for aisle or window seats?
5. What else did Wang Peng request?

**B.** Do a role play with a partner. One of you is a traveler, and the other is a travel agent. The traveler calls the travel agent to inquire about ticket prices from where he/she lives to Beijing, Hong Kong, or Taipei. As the traveler, you should tell the agent about your departure and return dates, the airlines you are interested in, and your preferences for seating and meals. As the agent, you should give the passenger a few different options and try to come to an agreement about his/her travel plans. (INTERPERSONAL)

**C.** Tell your classmates about a recent trip, your favorite trip, or a trip you would like to take in the future. Remember to mention the purpose of the trip, the dates, your transportation arrangements, your travel companions, the length of the trip, and any enjoyable or frustrating aspects of the trip. (PRESENTATIONAL)

# III. Reading Comprehension (INTERPRETIVE)

## A. Building Words

If you combine the *dān* in *dānchéng* with the *hào* in *hàomǎ*, you have *dānhào*, as seen in #1 below. Can you guess what the word *dānhào* means? Complete this section by providing the characters, the *pinyin*, and the English equivalent of each new word formed this way. You may consult a dictionary if necessary.

|  |  | new word | *pinyin* | English |
|---|---|---|---|---|
| 1. | "单程" 的 "单" + "号码" 的 "号" → 单+号 → | _____ | _____ | _____ |
| 2. | "往返" 的 "返" + "航班" 的 "航" → 返+航 → | _____ | _____ | _____ |
| 3. | "直飞" 的 "飞" + "糖醋鱼" 的 "鱼" → 飞+鱼 → | _____ | _____ | _____ |
| 4. | "转机" 的 "转" + "学校" 的 "学" → 转+学 → | _____ | _____ | _____ |
| 5. | "快慢" 的 "快" + "素餐" 的 "餐" → 快+餐 → | _____ | _____ | _____ |

xiāng

**B.** Read the passage and answer the questions.

　　小张和小蓝是男女朋友。小张常常换工作，什么工作钱多他就做什么工作，哪儿的工作好他就去哪儿住。他十个月前从北京搬到香港，可是在香港只住了半年多，就在上海找到了一个钱更多的工作。小蓝跟他不一样，对钱没有什么兴趣。哪个城市有文化她就喜欢哪个城市，所以她一直住在北京，哪儿也不想搬。小张说他每个星期都要坐飞机去北京看一次小蓝，把钱都花在飞机票上了，希望以后能两个星期飞一次。小蓝说要是小张爱她，又不想花钱，很简单，搬回北京。要不然，就再见。

Questions (True/False)

( )**1.** Little Zhang has lived in three different cities in the past year.

( )**2.** Little Zhang wants to experience life in different big cities.

( )**3.** Little Zhang makes more money now than he did months ago.

( )**4.** Little Lan is staying put because she has a well-paid job where she is.

( )**5.** Little Zhang is not happy about spending money on airline tickets.

( )**6.** Little Lan has given Little Zhang an ultimatum.

**C.** This is Teacher Gao's travel itinerary. Go over it and answer the questions in Chinese.

1. 你知道不知道高老师的飞机票是什么时候订的？

_____

2. 你知道不知道飞机票是多少钱买的？

_____

3. 高老师的飞机票是跟旅行社还是跟航空公司订的？

_____

4. 高老师哪一天走？从哪儿走？

_____

5. 高老师到什么地方去？

_____

6. 高老师哪一天回美国？

_____

7. 他回美国的航班号码是多少？

_____

8. 他买的是往返票还是单程票？

_____

9. 高老师去中国的时候坐的是直飞的飞机吗？

_____

10. 位子订好了吗？

_____

11. 旅行社的中文名字叫什么？

_____

**D.** Answer the following questions based on the menu.

午餐/晚餐

香港–北京

日本芥末苹果杂菜沙拉

欣
園
軒
*Yan Toh Heen*    黑椒汁扣牛肉配白饭

或

红酒烩猪柳配意大利面

*Häagen-Dazs*    哈根达斯雪糕

面包、牛油

*Pacific Coffee Company*    诚意提供　太平洋咖啡

福茗堂茶庄
*FOOK MING TONG Tea Shop*    福建乌龙、福建特级香片

红茶、日本绿茶

1.  This meal will be served on a flight between which two cities?_____

2.  Is this meal suitable for vegetarians? Why or why not?_____

3.  What beverages are available with the meal?_____

**E.** Look at the ad and answer the questions.

每逢 周四

图书 85折

音乐CD/DVD 9折

儿童幼教软体 85折

1.  Name two items that are on sale._____

2.  Which day of the week will customers get the discount?_____

**F.** Circle the baby bok choy. How much will you have to pay if the original price of the baby bok choy was $1?_____

What does 有机 mean?_____ (Hint: 有机 vegetables are more expensive than regular vegetables.)

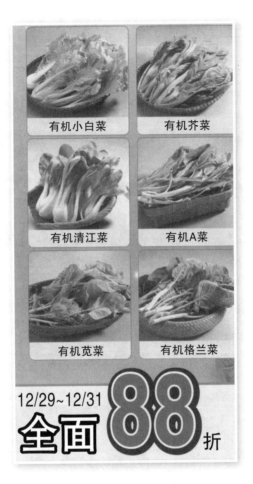

# IV. Writing Exercises

## A. Building Characters

Form a character by fitting the given components together as indicated. Then provide a word or phrase in which that character appears.

EXAMPLE: 左边一个"土"，右边一个"成了好朋友"的
"成"是__长城__的__城__。

1. 上边一个"窗户"的"户"，下边一个"方便"的
"方"是_____的_____。

2. 左边一个三点水，右边一个"台北"的"台"
是＿＿＿＿＿＿＿的＿＿＿＿。

3. 上边一个"夕"，下边一个"口"
是＿＿＿＿＿＿＿的＿＿＿＿。

4. 左边一个"汽车"的"车"，右边一个"专业"的
"专"是＿＿＿＿＿＿＿的＿＿＿＿。

5. 上边一个"广告"的"告"，下边一个"非常"的
"非"是＿＿＿＿＿＿＿的＿＿＿＿。

**B.** Search online to find out the population of the following cities, and express each city's population in Chinese.

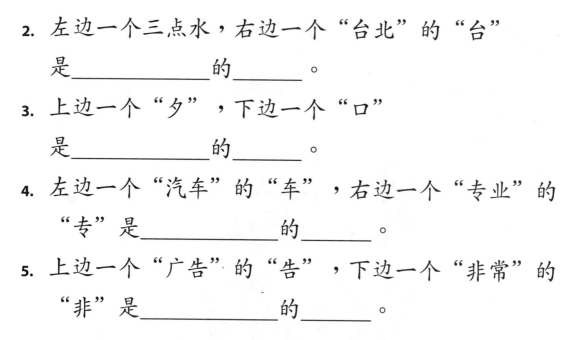

EXAMPLE:　香港　(about 7,000,000)

→香港差不多有七百万人。

1. 台北　　　　　→＿＿＿＿＿＿＿＿＿＿＿＿＿＿＿＿

2. 上海　　　　　→＿＿＿＿＿＿＿＿＿＿＿＿＿＿＿＿

3. 北京　　　　　→＿＿＿＿＿＿＿＿＿＿＿＿＿＿＿＿

4. 纽约　　　　　→＿＿＿＿＿＿＿＿＿＿＿＿＿＿＿＿

5. 东京　　　　　→＿＿＿＿＿＿＿＿＿＿＿＿＿＿＿＿

6. 我现在住的城市　→＿＿＿＿＿＿＿＿＿＿＿＿＿＿＿＿

**C.** First list the prices of the following items from two stores in Chinese. Then compare how much more or less expensive each item is at the two stores.

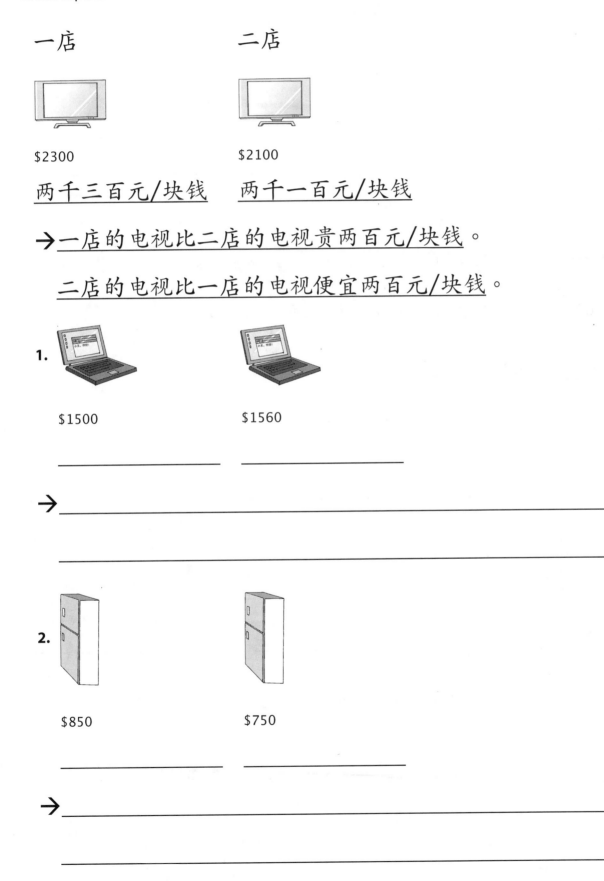

一店　　　　　　　　二店

$2300　　　　　　　　$2100

两千三百元/块钱　　两千一百元/块钱

→一店的电视比二店的电视贵两百元/块钱。

二店的电视比一店的电视便宜两百元/块钱。

1.

$1500　　　　　　　　$1560

_____ _____

→ _____

_____

2.

$850　　　　　　　　$750

_____ _____

→ _____

_____

**3.**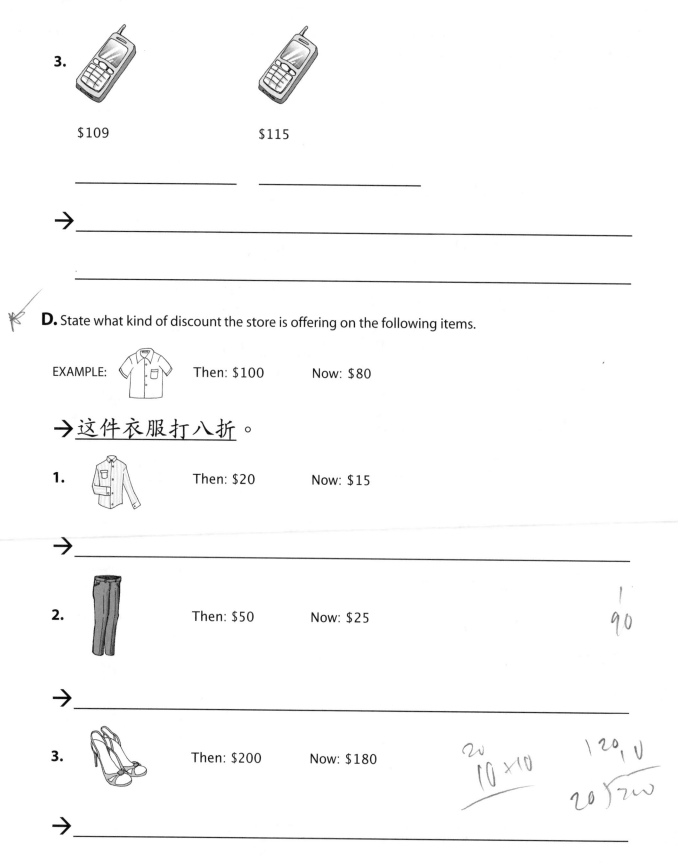

$109              $115

_____     _____

→ _____

_____

**D.** State what kind of discount the store is offering on the following items.

EXAMPLE:        Then: $100        Now: $80

→ <u>这件衣服打八折</u>。

**1.**        Then: $20        Now: $15

→ _____

**2.**        Then: $50        Now: $25

90

→ _____

**3.**        Then: $200        Now: $180

20
10 ×10        120, U

20 √2w

→ _____

**E.** Translate the following exchanges into Chinese. (PRESENTATIONAL)

1. **A:** Where would you like to sit?

   _____

   **B:** I'll sit wherever you would like to.

   _____

   **A:** Let's sit next to the window. What would you like to drink?

   _____

   **B:** I'll have whatever you order.

   _____

   **A:** What kind of dishes would you like to have?

   _____

   **B:** I'll eat anything.

   _____

2. **A:** I heard that airline tickets are on sale.

   _____

   **B:** I'll go online and check right now.

   _____

   **A:** Twenty percent off or thirty percent off?

   _____

   **B:** The online ad says that if you buy a round-trip ticket, the second round-trip ticket will be fifty percent off.

   _____

   _____

   **A:** Then forget it.

   _____

**F.** Imagine that you are a travel agent who just helped a customer plan her trip and book her airline tickets. Now you are going to go over the itinerary with the customer in Chinese, since she does not understand English. Be as detailed as possible, and include information such as when and where she is departing and returning, the route she is taking, how long each flight will take, the airlines she is taking, the flight numbers, whether the tickets are one-way or round-trip, whether the flights are nonstop, etc. (芝加哥 Zhījiāgē, 洛杉矶 Luòshānjī) (PRESENTATIONAL)

| Southwest Airlines Air Itinerary | | | | | | |
|---|---|---|---|---|---|---|
| Trip | Date | Day | Stops | Routing | Flight | Routing Details |
| Depart | Jul 15 | Sat | N/S | MDW–LAX | 971 | Depart Chicago (MDW) at 1:05 PM Arrive in Los Angeles (LAX) at 3:20 PM |
| Return | Aug 04 | Fri | N/S | LAX–MDW | 723 | Depart Los Angeles (LAX) at 10:20 AM Arrive in Chicago (MDW) at 4:15 PM |

## G. Storytelling

Write a story based on the four illustrations below. Make sure that your story has a beginning, middle and end. Also make sure that the transition from one picture to the next is smooth and logical.
(PRESENTATIONAL)

酒店　　　机票　　　旅游　　　商旅

These are the services offered by a travel agency. Can you recognize some of the services?

# 20

## LESSON 20   At the Airport
### 第二十课 在机场

## PART ONE    Dialogue I: Checking In at the Airport

### 💿 I. Listening Comprehension

**A. Textbook Dialogue** (Multiple Choice) (INTERPRETIVE)

( )  **1.** How many people are seeing Wang Peng and Li You off at the airport?

   **a.** two
   **b.** three
   **c.** four
   **d.** five

( )  **2.** When did Wang Peng and Li You finish checking in?

   **a.** around 9:00
   **b.** around 10:00
   **c.** around 11:00
   **d.** around 12:00

( )  **3.** What will Bai Ying'ai be doing while Wang Peng and Li You are traveling?

   **a.** interning in New York
   **b.** going back home
   **c.** going to California with Gao Wenzhong
   **d.** joining Wang Peng and Li You in Beijing

( )  **4.** Wang Hong will be_____.

   **a.** all by herself
   **b.** with Gao Xiaoyin
   **c.** traveling with Gao Wenzhong and Bai Ying'ai
   **d.** going back to China in a few weeks

### B. Workbook Narrative (True/False) (INTERPRETIVE)

( ) **1.** The speaker is likely an airline ground crew member.

( ) **2.** The flight is from Beijing to Shanghai.

( ) **3.** The plane will arrive at the destination at 3:00 pm.

( ) **4.** No snacks or beverages will be served because it is a short flight.

### C. Listening Rejoinder (INTERPERSONAL)

In this section, you will hear two speakers talking. After hearing the first speaker, select the best from the four possible responses given by the second speaker.

_____

# II. Speaking Exercises

**A.** Answer the questions in Chinese based on the Textbook Dialogue. (INTERPRETIVE/PRESENTATIONAL)

1. How many pieces of luggage did Wang Peng check?

2. Where should Wang Peng and Li You go to board the plane?

3. Why did Wang Hong sound worried?

4. What will Bai Ying'ai do this summer?

5. What did Li You say when she learned about Bai Ying'ai and Gao Wenzhong's summer plans?

6. What did Bai Ying'ai tell Wang Peng and Li You to do when they arrived in Beijing?

**B.** In Chinese, what do people usually say when they see their friends off? (PRESENTATIONAL)

**C.** Work with two or three people on a role play. Imagine you are at the local airport seeing your friend(s) off. Have a small talk right before the departure of your friend(s). (INTERPERSONAL)

# III. Reading Comprehension (INTERPRETIVE)

## A. Building Words

If you combine the *shū* in *shūdiàn* with *bāo*, you have *shūbāo*, as seen in #1 below. Can you guess what the word *shūbāo* means? Complete this section by providing the characters, the *pinyin*, and the English equivalent of each new word formed this way. You may consult a dictionary if necessary.

|  | new word | *pinyin* | English |
|---|---|---|---|

1. "书店"的"书"＋"包"

   → 书＋包 → _____ _____ _____

2. "超重"的"超"＋"汽车"的"车"

   → 超＋车 → _____ _____ _____

3. "超重"的"超"＋"高速公路"的"速"

   → 超＋速 → _____ _____ _____

4. "汽车"的"车"＋"登机牌"的"牌"

   → 车＋牌 → _____ _____ _____

5. "出去"的"出"＋"登机口"的"口"

   → 出＋口 → _____ _____ _____

**B.** Read the passage and answer the questions.

　　今天白英爱坐飞机回学校。她托运了一件大行李，然后带着一个小包，护照和登机牌到九号登机口上飞机。上了飞机以后，白英爱刚在自己的位子上坐下，就听到航空公司的一位女服务员跟大家说："这是去纽约的521号航班。要是您上错了飞机，请您赶快下飞机。"她刚说完，坐在白英爱旁边的两位先生就说："不对！我们的航班是去纽约的，可是是531号！"女服务员听了以后，就和另外一位服务员一起到飞机的前边去了。五分钟以后，她才回来对大家说："真对不起，你们是对的，这是531号航班。我们上错飞机了。"

Questions (True/False)

( )  **1.** Bai Ying'ai had two pieces of baggage.

( )  **2.** Bai Ying'ai went to the wrong boarding gate.

( )  **3.** The men sitting next to Bai Ying'ai realized that they had boarded the wrong airplane.

( )  **4.** Both Flight 521 and Flight 531 were bound for New York.

( )  **5.** We can assume that Bai Ying'ai will not see that attendant during her flight.

**C.** Read the dialogue and answer the questions. (True/False)

高文中：英爱！

白英爱：文中！等了很久吧？飞机一个小时以前就到了，可是我等托运的行李等了半天了还没等到。

高文中：真的？航空公司一定是把你的行李放错飞机了。别担心，他们会找到的。

白英爱：他们告诉我行李到了会给我打电话，要我等他们的电话。还好，我的信用卡、护照、钱，都在这个小包里，要不然就麻烦了。下一班飞机是两点半到，我想我的包一定在那个飞机上。我们还得等一个多小时。

高文中：那我们找个地方喝点咖啡吧。你知道吗，李友后天要跟王朋一起去北京。

白英爱：是吗？那我们后天可以去送他们。对了，我还没告诉李友我们要去加州，她可能以为我要去纽约实习呢。

……

(航空公司的电话)：白英爱小姐吗？非常对不起，我们刚查到您托运的行李，您的行李现在正在去东京的飞机上…

( )1. 白英爱的航班早到了一个小时。

( )2. 白英爱花了两个半小时找她的行李，可是没有找到。

( )3. 高文中觉得白英爱的行李在别的飞机上。

( )4. 白英爱很担心她托运的包，因为她的护照在那个包里。

( )5. 白英爱早就知道李友要和王朋一起去北京。

( )6. 李友还不知道白英爱最新的暑假计划。

( )7. 白英爱一个多小时以后能拿到她托运的行李。

**D.** The following is a notice posted in an airport. Will it help people locate their luggage, airlines, or boarding gates?

_____

## IV. Writing Exercises

**A.** Fill in the blanks with either 的, 得, or 地.

　　暑假快到了，大家都高高兴兴_____准备放假，有的人打算去旅行，有的人打算去实习。但也有的人什么事都不想做，只想好好儿_____在家休息休息。

　　希望每个人_____暑假都过_____很好，下个学期再见。

**B.** Fill in the blanks with either 的时候 or 以后.

1. 生病_____，别乱跑，得在家休息。

2. 父母死了_____，都是大哥在照顾我们。

3. 开车_____，别打手机，太危险了。

4. 行李超重_____得多付钱。

5. 签证办好_____，就可以订机票了。

**C.** Translate the following exchanges into Chinese. (PRESENTATIONAL)

1. **A:** Be careful. This place is dangerous. Don't run around.

   _____

   **B:** Don't worry. I'm sitting right here.

   _____

2. **A:** Don't forget to send me an e-mail when you get to Tokyo.

   _____

   **B:** OK... Don't cry. I'll be back in a month. Study hard at school.

   _____

   **A:** OK. Goodbye. Have fun.

   _____

**D.** Let's plan a trip to China. Choose two cities in China that you would like to visit. First explain why you're interested in these two cities, and then arrange your route from your current location. Search online for information about the cities, airfares, and hotel accommodations, and put together a travel itinerary. Your travel itinerary needs to include all the information on the flights, the airlines, the airfares, the time it will take to get to each destination and the time you plan to spend there, things you need to take care of before you depart, things you need to take with you on the trip, and your transportation to and from the airports. Don't forget to keep an eye on your budget. (PRESENTATIONAL)

**E.** Your friend from China is planning to travel within the United States and needs your help to understand the airline's rule. Use the information below to explain to your friend all the rules about luggage on this particular airline.

(pound: 磅, bàng) (PRESENTATIONAL)

---

**Domestic Free Luggage Allowance**

Each ticketed passenger traveling domestically is allowed one piece of checked luggage and one piece of carry-on luggage plus a purse or briefcase or laptop case. All checked and carry-on luggage is subject to the following limitations:

**Checked Luggage**

The Airline will accept checked luggage up to a maximum weight of 50 pounds (23kg). Luggage weighing between 50 and 70 pounds (23-32kg) will be assessed $25 USD per piece and luggage weighing between 70 and 100 pounds (32-46kg) will be assessed $50 USD per piece. Luggage weighing over 100 pounds (46kg) will not be accepted as checked luggage.

**Carry-On Luggage**

Each person is allowed to carry onboard the aircraft one piece of luggage. This piece of luggage must not exceed 40 pounds. In addition to this one piece of carry-on luggage, customers may also carry onboard a purse or briefcase or laptop computer. In addition, each passenger may carry a coat, umbrella, or other "special" items.

---

班次＝班机＝航班

## PART TWO   Dialogue II: Arriving in Beijing

## I. Listening Comprehension

### A. Textbook Dialogue (True/False) (INTERPRETIVE)

( ) **1.** Wang Peng's grandparents are waiting in the car outside the airport terminal.

( ) **2.** Wang Peng's parents are impressed with Li You's Chinese.

( ) **3.** Wang Peng has lost some weight due to his busy schedule.

( ) **4.** Wang Peng's parents plan to take Wang Peng and Li You directly home.

### B. Workbook Narrative (True/False) (INTERPRETIVE)

Li You called her father from Beijing. Choose the best answers to the questions after listening to the message she left for him.

( ) **1.** Where is Li You?

    **a.** in a roast duck restaurant

    **b.** at the airport terminal

    **c.** at Wang Peng's parents' apartment

    **d.** in the car leaving the airport

( ) **2.** Li You promises to_____.

    **a.** call her dad again tomorrow

    **b.** catch up on her sleep

    **c.** buy a cell phone for her father

    **d.** buy some DVDs for her father

( ) **3.** Li You is_____.

    **a.** very tired

    **b.** homesick already

    **c.** impressed with the Beijing airport

    **d.** very impatient

( ) **4.** Li You is calling from_____.

    **a.** Wang Peng's cell phone

    **b.** Wang Peng's dad's cell phone

    **c.** Wang Peng's mom's cell phone

    **d.** her own cell phone

## C. Listening Rejoinder (INTERPERSONAL)

In this section, you will hear two speakers talking. After hearing the first speaker, select the best from the four possible responses given by the second speaker.

_____

# II. Speaking Exercises

**A.** Answer the questions in Chinese based on the Textbook Dialogue. (INTERPRETIVE/PRESENTATIONAL)

1. How did Li You address Wang Peng's parents?

2. How did Li You account for her Chinese language skills?

3. Wang Peng's mother thought that Wang Peng had lost some weight. What did she think was the reason?

4. What did Wang Peng say about how Wang Hong was doing in the United States?

5. Where were Wang Peng's grandparents?

**B.** What would you say to someone who compliments you on your Chinese? (PRESENTATIONAL)

**C.** Do a role play with two classmates. You are traveling with a Chinese friend and meeting his/her parent for the first time at an airport in China or Taiwan. Make up a conversation for the meeting. Address your host parent appropriately, and express your feelings about your flight. The Chinese friend should make sure to introduce everyone. The parent should ask you about the trip, what you would like to do on your visit, etc. (INTERPERSONAL)

# III. Reading Comprehension (INTERPRETIVE)

## A. Building Words

If you combine the *kǎo* in *kǎoyā* with the *ròu* in *niúròu*, you have *kǎo ròu*, as seen in #1 below. Can you guess what the word *kǎo ròu* means? Complete this section by providing the characters, the *pinyin*, and the English equivalent of each new word formed this way. You may consult a dictionary if necessary.

|  | new word | *pinyin* | English |
|---|---|---|---|

1. "烤鸭" 的 "烤" + "牛肉" 的 "肉"

   → 烤+肉 → _____     _____     _____

2. "烤鸭" 的 "烤" + "箱子" 的 "箱"

   → 烤+箱 → _____     _____     _____

3. "烤鸭" 的 "鸭" + "蛋糕" 的 "蛋"

→　鸭+蛋　→　_____　_____　_____

4. "一块钱" 的 "钱" + "包"

→　钱+包　→　_____　_____　_____

5. "海" + "托运" 的 "运"

→　海+运　→　_____　_____　_____

**B.** Read the passage and answer the questions.

　　王朋的妹妹王红来美国找王朋的时候，她的爸爸、妈妈、爷爷和奶奶都到机场去送她。因为王红的行李太多了，她爸爸的汽车放不下，所以爸爸跟妈妈开他们自己的车，王红跟爷爷奶奶坐出租汽车去机场。因为这是王红第一次出国，所以爸爸妈妈都很担心，一直告诉她到美国以后要好好照顾自己。妈妈要王红一到美国就让哥哥给家里打电话。王红知道哥哥在美国一年了，有很多朋友，他们会照顾她的。她真不懂爸爸妈妈为什么这么担心。

Questions (True/False)

( ) 1. 王红去美国的时候不是坐爸爸的汽车去机场的。

( ) 2. 王红去美国以前去过一次日本。

( ) 3. 王朋比王红早一年去美国。

( ) 4. 王红到美国以后就会打电话给爸爸妈妈。

( ) 5. 王红出国，爸爸妈妈比王红自己更担心。

**C.** Read the passage and answer the questions.

王红在高小音家住了三个月了，英文水平提高了不少。王红说都是因为小音教得好，可是小音说是因为王红聪明。为了谢谢小音照顾自己，王红计划秋天请小音跟她一起去北京，带小音看看北京的名胜古迹，当小音的导游，还要请她吃北京烤鸭。为了准备去中国，小音这几天每天都跟王红说中文，希望自己中文越来越好，秋天去中国什么都听得懂，什么都会说。

Questions (True/False)

( ) **1.** Wang Hong is quite modest about her English studies.

( ) **2.** Gao Xiaoyin is not satisfied with Wang Hong's English progress.

( ) **3.** Wang Hong wants to go back to Beijing in the fall because she's homesick.

( ) **4.** Wang Hong plans to hire a tour guide for Gao Xiaoyin.

( ) **5.** Gao Xiaoyin thinks her own Chinese is perfect.

**D.** Give the *pinyin* of the sentence seen here.

# IV. Writing Exercises

## A. Building Characters

Form a character by fitting the given components together as indicated. Then provide a word or phrase in which that character appears.

EXAMPLE: 左边一个"力气"的"力"，右边一个"登机口"的"口"是 <u>"加州"</u> 的 <u>"加"</u> 。

1. 上边一个"木"，下边一个"子"是 _____ 的 _____ 。

2. 左边一个足字旁，右边一个"包"是 _____ 的 _____ 。

3. 左边一个人字旁，右边一个"牛肉"的"牛"是 _____ 的 _____ 。

4. 上边一个"田"，下边一个"糸"是 _____ 的 _____ 。

5. 左边一个"火"，右边一个"考试"的"考"是 _____ 的 _____ 。

**B.** Answer the following questions. (PRESENTATIONAL)

1. 要是在机场或者车站送人，你会说些什么话？

   _____

   _____

   _____

2. 要是在机场或者车站接人，你会说些什么话？

_____

_____

_____

**C.** Translate the following into Chinese. (PRESENTATIONAL)

1. **A:** You've worked for more than ten hours. You must be exhausted.

   _____

   **B:** I'm all right.

   _____

   **A:** You haven't had any food for eight hours. You must be starving.

   _____

   **B:** I'm OK.

2. **A:** I eat whatever you eat and drink whatever you drink. How come I'm getting fatter and fatter and you're getting thinner and thinner?

   _____

   **B:** I exercise two or three times a week. How about you? You haven't exercised for two years.

   _____

3. Wang Peng emailed Wang Hong from Beijing. See if you can translate his email.

Sister:

We arrived in Beijing yesterday afternoon. We waited a long time for our checked luggage. Mom and Dad came to the airport to pick us up. Li You and I felt all right. We weren't too tired. As soon as we got out of the airport, we headed straight for the Peking duck restaurant for dinner. When we arrived at the restaurant, Grandma and Grandpa were already there. I hadn't had Peking duck for a long time, and enjoyed the food very much. Li You is a vegetarian, so she didn't have duck, and only had some vegetable dumplings. She ate faster than Grandma and Grandpa, and after she finished her food, she said in Chinese to Grandma and Grandpa: "Take time with the food." I think Grandma and Grandpa were happy after hearing that.

Your brother

_____

_____

_____

_____

_____

_____

_____

_____

**D.** Use the pictures to help you describe what people normally do: 1) one month before traveling overseas, 2) on the night before flying out, and 3) on the day of traveling. (PRESENTATIONAL)

1. _____

2. _____

3. _____

**E.** Pick a tourist/historical site in Beijing or another major Chinese-speaking city that you would like to visit. Search online for information on the site. Write a simple tourist pamphlet, including information on where it is located (east, south, west, or north of the city), how far it is from the airport, what transportation people can use to get there, why it is famous, etc. Don't forget to provide the pinyin and the characters for the name of the site. (PRESENTATIONAL)

## F. Family Tree

Draw your family tree and list your family members and close relatives in Chinese. Use Grammar 4 in the textbook as a reference to complete the tree. (PRESENTATIONAL)

父亲          母亲

我

# G. Storytelling (PRESENTATIONAL)

Write a story based on the four cartoons below. Make sure that your story has a beginning, middle and end. Also make sure that the transition from one picture to the next is smooth and logical.

# Let's Review (LESSONS 16–20)

## I. How do you say these words/phrases?

Write down their correct pronunciation and tones in *pinyin*, and use a tape recorder or computer to record them. Hand in the recording to your teacher if asked.

1. 我们俩 我们两个 _____ _____

2. 出租　厨房　　叔叔 _____ _____ _____

3. 家具　公寓　　旅行 _____ _____ _____

4. 不准　不瘦　　难受 _____ _____ _____

5. 导游　游泳　 _____ _____

6. 书架　暑假　 _____ _____

## II. Group the characters according to their radicals, and provide the meaning of each radical.

架　初　简　特　跑　胖　椅　被
篮　物　桌　脚　踢　签　棒　脸

| Radical | Meaning of the Radical (English) | Characters |
|---------|----------------------------------|------------|
| 1. _____ | _____ | _____ |
| 2. _____ | _____ | _____ |
| 3. _____ | _____ | _____ |
| 4. _____ | _____ | _____ |
| 5. _____ | _____ | _____ |
| 6. _____ | _____ | _____ |

## III. VO or Not

Among the verbs below, distinguish those that are VO compounds from those that are not.

打扫　　　整理　　　旅行　　　做饭　　　走路　　　游泳

跑步　　　放假　　　实习　　　打工　　　转机　　　托运

**VO Compounds:** _____

**not VO Compounds:** _____

## IV. Have You Seen that Character Before?

Circle the character shared by the words in each group. Write down the *pinyin* for the character in common, and define the character's original meaning.

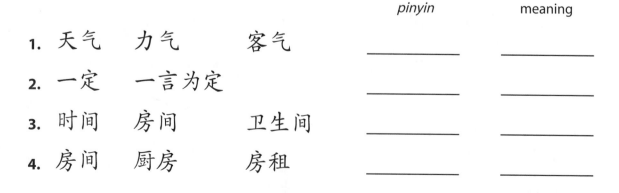

|  |  |  |  | *pinyin* | meaning |
|--|--|--|--|----------|---------|
| 1. 天气 | 力气 | 客气 | | _____ | _____ |
| 2. 一定 | 一言为定 | | | _____ | _____ |
| 3. 时间 | 房间 | 卫生间 | | _____ | _____ |
| 4. 房间 | 厨房 | 房租 | | _____ | _____ |

| | | | | |
|---|---|---|---|---|
| 5. | 预报 | 报纸 | | _____ _____ |
| 6. | 最近 | 附近 | | _____ _____ |
| 7. | 分钟 | 钟头 | | _____ _____ |
| 8. | 教室 | 卧室 | 办公室 | _____ _____ |
| 9. | 请客 | 客气 | 客厅 | _____ _____ |
| 10. | 餐厅 | 客厅 | | _____ _____ |
| 11. | 暑期班 | 暑假 | | _____ _____ |
| 12. | 礼物 | 宠物 | | _____ _____ |
| 13. | 发音 | 发烧 | 发短信 | _____ _____ |
| 14. | 平常 | 水平 | 平安 | _____ _____ |
| 15. | 平安 | 安静 | | _____ _____ |
| 16. | 网上 | 网球 | | _____ _____ |
| 17. | 保险 | 危险 | | _____ _____ |
| 18. | 高兴 | 兴趣 | | _____ _____ |
| 19. | 名字 | 有名 | 名胜古迹 | _____ _____ |
| 20. | 寒假 | 暑假 | 放假 | _____ _____ |
| 21. | 办法 | 怎么办 | 办公室 | _____ _____ |
| 22. | 长城 | 城市 | 中国城 | _____ _____ |
| 23. | 简单 | 单程 | | _____ _____ |
| 24. | 告訴 | 广告 | | _____ _____ |
| 25. | 走路 | 走道 | | _____ _____ |
| 26. | 运动 | 托运 | | _____ _____ |
| 27. | 喜欢 | 欢迎 | | _____ _____ |

28. 起床　起飞 　　　　　　　　　—————

29. 公司　公寓　　公园　　　　公共汽车　　高速公路

　　　　　　　　　　　　　　　　—————　　　—————

30. 学习　练习　　预习　　　　复习　　　实习

　　　　　　　　　　　　　　　　—————　　　—————

## V. Getting to Know You

Put your Chinese to use. Interview one of your classmates to find out more about him/her. After a brief Q & A session, jot down and organize the information you have gathered, and then present an oral or written report to introduce your classmate to others. (INTERPERSONAL/PRESENTATIONAL)

### A: Are you a sports fan?

1. 你对什么运动有兴趣？

2. 你对什么球赛有兴趣？

3. 你平常运动吗？

　　✓　a. 你每个星期运动几次？每次运动多长时间？

　　✗　b. 你多长时间没运动了？

4. 你觉得什么运动最简单？为什么？

5. 你觉得什么运动最麻烦？为什么？

6. 你觉得什么运动最危险？为什么？

### B: Should I move or should I stay?

1. 你住的地方是宿舍、公寓、还是房子？住得下三个人吗？

2. 你住的地方几房几厅？有没有自己的厨房、卫生间？

3. 你住的地方带不带家具？有什么家具？

4. 你觉得你的房间干净吗？你常常整理房间吗？

5. 你每个月打扫几次房子？

6. 这个地方对你合适吗？为什么？

7. 你打算住下去还是搬出去？为什么？

## C. Do you like to travel?

1. 你去过哪些城市/国家？

2. 你对哪一个城市/国家的印象最好/最糟糕？

3. 你是什么时候去的？怎么去的？

4. 你在那儿玩儿了多长时间？

5. 你还会再去一次吗？

6. 如果你有钱、有时间，你希望能到什么地方去旅行？

7. 要是坐飞机，你怎么订票？你跟旅行社、航空公司订机票，还是上网订机票？

# VI. Beijing vs. New York City

Both Beijing and New York City are big cities. Search online and find out more about the two cities. Compare the two, and see how similar or different they are. You can take on all six tasks or choose just a few. (INTERPRETIVE/PRESENTATIONAL)

## 1. Weather

Check the weather forecast for tomorrow for the two cities. Compare which city will be warmer or colder and whether it's supposed to rain tomorrow.

## 2. Population

List the population of the two cities. Then compare which city has more people.

## 3. Transportation

Find out what means of public transportation are available in each city and compare which public transportation system is more convenient. Figure out where the international airports are located in relation to the downtown area, and how to get to them.

## 4. Shopping

List today's currency exchange rate for U.S. dollars and RMB. Find out how much a watermelon, a refrigerator, and a basketball would cost in a local store in each city. Compare the prices between the two cities.

## 5. Housing

List today's currency exchange rate for U.S. dollars and RMB. Find out how much it would cost to rent an apartment with two bedrooms and one bathroom in each city.

## 6. Traveling

Find one US airline and one Chinese airline that provide flight service between the two cities. Describe the route they take, the times the flights depart, the flight time, the airfares, how many meals they serve onboard, etc. Compare the two options, and figure out which airline has better ticket prices, a shorter flight time, and better service.